DEVOTION TO OUR LADY

THE MARIAN LIFE AS TAUGHT BY THE SAINTS

Fr. Stefano Maria Manelli, FI
Minister General and Founder of the Franciscans of the Immaculate

Academy of the Immaculate
New Bedford, MA
2001

Devotion to Our Lady is a book prepared for publication by the Franciscans of the Immaculate [marymediatrix.com], POB 3003, New Bedford, MA, 02741-3003. Translator: Rev. Fr. Alphonsus Mary Sutton, FI, STD, revised by Fr. Maximilian Mary Dean, FI, from the original Italian *La Devozione alla Madonna.*

Imprimatur   Most. Rev. Sean Patrick O'Malley
                      OFM Cap., Bishop of Fall River
                      Massachusetts, USA
                      September 15, 2001
                      Feast of the Sorrowful Mother

The Imprimatur is a declaration of the Roman Catholic Church that the work is free from error in matters of faith and morals; but in no way does it imply that she endorses the contents of the work.

ISBN: 978-1-60114-018-0

– *Third Printing, December 2011* –

CONTENTS

CHAPTER III

HOW IS DEVOTION TO OUR LADY LIVED?

DEDICATION

We humbly venture to make our own the following sentiments that St. Alphonsus Mary De Liguori expresses in the Dedication of his wonderful book *The Glories of Mary*:

"My beloved Redeemer and Lord Jesus Christ, because I know the pleasure it gives You when someone seeks to glorify Your most Holy Mother, whom You love so much and whom you so greatly desire to see loved and honored by all, I have chosen to publish this book that tells of her glories.

"I know of no one to whom I can better entrust the care of this work than You, Who has such great zeal for Your Mother's glory. Therefore I dedicate and recommend it to You. Take it under Your protection and cause it to shed on all readers, the light to have confidence in this Immaculate Virgin, and let it set them afire with love for her, whom You have redeemed. In return for this poor labor of mine, I beg You to grant me that love for Mary which, in writing this book, I have wished to see enkindled in all its readers."

FOREWORD

"We are happier than Our Lady, because she… did not have a Blessed Virgin to love!…"

This pleasing banter of the Little Flower, St. Therese, should not leave us unmoved. What surprising beauty it contains! It enables us to see in a flash the charming quality of love for Our Lady. It makes us understand in an instant the happiness we miss if we have no devotion to Our Lady.

St. Maximilian Mary Kolbe, the great "fool for the Immaculate," used to say with ardor: "Dear sons, if you want to live and die happy, work to develop a deep filial love for our dear heavenly Mother."

Here we have the aim of this booklet: To cast a bit of light on the beauty and value of devotion to Our Lady; to awaken a bit of enthusiasm for imitating the life and the virtues of this holy Woman; — and all this according to the teachings and examples given by our favorite models, the saints. May God grant that at least some souls may come to understand the value and importance of devotion to Our Lady!

One day a friar asked St. Pio of Pietrelcina, "Father, what are your thoughts about Our Lady?" He replied, "She is worth more than theology and philosophy."

This answer of Padre Pio echoes the words of the Holy Spirit which the liturgy places upon the lips of Our Lady: *"I encircled the vault of the sky, and I walked on the bottom of the deep"* (Ec 24:5). What a vast and heavenly reality is the mystery of Mary!

She is *our* Lady. She belongs to God and to mankind. She is both Jesus' Mother and ours. *"Behold, thy son"* (Jn 19:26). Our Lady cannot fail to love us. Motherhood signifies love. If St. Paul found his *"daily preoccupation"* to be *"anxiety for all the churches"* (2 Cor 11:28), how much more are all of us the concern of Our Lady, who is Mother of us all? The holy Curé of Ars ventured to say that not even in Heaven can Our Lady enjoy Paradise in peace; for she is like a good mother with children away from home who is watching out for their return. Her cares will cease only at the end of time when her last child shall enter the Father's house and she, having at last her children about her, will be able to enjoy her Paradise in peace.

How do we respond to the love of this good heavenly Mother? Do we desire to honor her with gratitude? Have we sentiments of love for her as our Mother? Are we, like true children, striving to be like her? *"Behold, thy Mother!"* (Jn 19:27). If Our Lady is our Mother, it is clear that *"the Church's devotedness to the Virgin Mary is an intrinsic element of the Christian Religion,"* and that we *"cannot be Christians without being Marian,"* according to Pope Paul VI's beautiful statement.

The more Marian we are, the more Christian we are. The more fully we belong to Our Lady, the more Jesus will claim us as His own. The more we resemble the Mother of God, the more we will resemble our divine Brother, Jesus, *"Son of the virginity"* of Mary (St. Ambrose). Becoming true *images of Jesus* in Mary is the genuine fruit of devotion to Our Lady (cf. Rom 8:29).

As St. John the Evangelist, in receiving Our Lady, *"took her into his own"* (Jn 19:27), so may it be granted us to welcome Our Lady in the dwelling of our hearts.

If we do not have a true Marian devotion, then we ought to beg for it as did St. Francis de Sales: "My God, when shall we have the grace that the Holy Virgin might be born in our hearts?"

But if we already have the grace of devotion to Our Lady, we should apply all zeal and every effort for its increase, since salvation and sanctification depend on Our Lady's living presence in our lives as well as in the life of the whole Church. "Mary," declared St. Bernard, "is the whole reason for our hope." St. Louis Grignon de Montfort preached the same. St. Alphonsus M. Liguori taught likewise; and this was the firm conviction of St. John Bosco: in a famous dream he saw a ship, representing the Church, standing firm and victorious in the midst of the tempest because it was anchored to two immovable pillars — the Eucharist and the Immaculate.

Our Lady saves us. Our Lady gives us life. Our Lady enriches us with God. With the Holy Spirit she repeats to us: *"He who finds me, finds life, and will have salvation from the Lord"* (Pr 8:35). And again: *"With me are riches and glory ... that I may enrich them that love me"* (Pr 8:18, 21). It was not without reason that St. Pius X proposed devotion to Our Lady as a primary means to restore all things to Christ in the Church and in the world.

Let us, then, love Our Lady. We make our own the last recommendation of St. Pio of Pietrelcina: "Love Our Lady and bring others to love her. Always recite the Rosary." Let us love Our Lady without ever saying we have loved her enough; rather, let us promote a holy rivalry in order to be the generation giving the most glory to Mary (cf. Lk 1:48).

Once, St. Maximilian M. Kolbe received encouragement from some confreres who expressed the hope that he always increase in love for the Immaculate Virgin. The Saint replied by thanking them and extended to them his desire that they might surpass him in love for Our Lady a thousand times, and that he might then, in turn, surpass them a million times, while they, in turn, might then surpass him a billion times; and he desired that this worthy competition might continue in this fashion without ever ceasing.

We want to extend to every reader this same desire that St. Maximilian expressed: may you surpass every limit in filial love for "our dear heavenly Mother."

"He who finds Me finds life."

(Pr 8:35)

Chapter I

WHAT IS DEVOTION TO OUR LADY?

- ◆ **Being Sons and Daughters of Mary**

- ◆ **Being Jesus for Mary**

- ◆ **Being Mary for Jesus**

BEING SONS AND DAUGHTERS OF MARY

Once I happened to hear this brief conversation between a little girl and her pastor, who was an elderly priest:

"What is devotion to Our Lady?" the little girl naïvely inquired.

"It is the gift of oneself to Our Lady," the priest answered promptly.

How beautifully both the question and answer were put! I was struck with the shortness and completeness of it. The essential thing was very simply told. I doubt that it could have been expressed better in so few words.

St. Thomas Aquinas tells us that true devotion consists in a "prompt and complete gift of one's entire self." The word *devotion* indicates a *giving*, or better, a *giving of self*. This is not, of course, just any giving of self, but giving with love, with generosity, with delight.

Therefore, my devotion to Our Lady ought to consist in *a loving bestowal of myself to Our Lady*; that is, I should make a gift of myself to her. And if one who receives a gift can do with it what he wishes, then Our Lady can do whatever she wants with me, her gift, and I cannot do anything other than what she wants, what she finds pleasing, what she is effecting. The more devoted I am to Our Lady, the more I surrender myself to her and adjust my ways to suit her wishes, living in all respects under her guidance.

Marian devotion thus understood, in its fuller and more perfect sense, requires the *consecration* of oneself to Our Lady; that is, the explicit offering to Mary of one's whole being, of all that one is and all that one has — soul, body, senses; external goods, internal goods, present and future goods; one's life, one's death, and one's eternity.

With a consecration made in this way one reaches the fullness of devotion to Our Lady because, in every way, he is truly *given* to Our Lady and unconditionally belongs to her; and one makes the choice to live, without reservation, as her child, either to be her "slave of love" (St. Louis Grignon de Montfort), or, to go further, to make himself her "property, an instrument within her hands" (St. Maximilian M. Kolbe), or — going even further — one offers himself as a "victim of holocaust" in honor of her motherly and merciful love and for the coming of God's kingdom into all souls.

On these pages we will speak of devotion to Our Lady that ranges from the lowest to the highest degree of perfection. We will use simply the word devotion, at times referring to the early stages of Marian *devotion* and, at times, to its fully developed, perfect stage which is consecration. Our essential aim is that all may begin having this devotion, or, if they have it, that they may proceed to improve it and cultivate it as a heavenly garden of loving service to Our Lady, a garden which has been tended by all the saints.

As Jesus did

The supreme example of devotion to Our Lady is something we receive from no one else than God himself. God was the one who first gave himself to Mary. He gave himself to her in so perfect a manner as to become her Son. In this way Jesus was the first and greatest client of Mary.

"But wait just a minute… Huh, I never thought of it like that before!… Yet it is precisely the truth!…" so exclaimed one soul who was dumbfounded upon hearing this reflection.

Yes, it is absolutely true. God Himself has set the greatest example, one which has infinite value and infinite beauty. If we consider that nothing else can belong to a creature in quite the same way that a son belongs to his parent, we can then comprehend what Jesus' devotion to Mary was like, and what ours ought to be.

Now, we must be *"imitators of God,"* as St. Paul tells us (Eph 5:1). We ought to be *"conformed to Jesus"* (cf. Rom 8:29). And St. Maximilian Kolbe, that fool who was so enamored of the Immaculate, has written in our time that "the imitation of Jesus is our whole sanctity."

If God, then, gave himself to Mary to the extent of becoming her Child, so we too ought to give ourselves to Mary so as to become her children. We, too, are to be children of Mary, like Jesus, our divine Model — we, her children by grace; Jesus, her Child by nature.

There is a lovely poem in which St. Thérèse of Lisieux describes the happy impression she experienced when dwelling on this sweet truth: Jesus and Thérèse are children of the same Mother; and it is our happy lot, our happy office, to imitate Jesus in His role as a child of Mary.

And this is necessary; for otherwise our conformity to Jesus would lack "a fundamental element," as Pope Pius XII declares. One cannot resemble Jesus if one does not have Mary as His Mother, or if one shows himself cold and indifferent to her. For that would be something we could not admit.

This reflection should be enough for us to understand how devotion to Our Lady is, beyond doubt, necessary for our sanctification, for our full conformity to Jesus.

If we add that Our Lady is the way to the Savior for us, that is to say, our path to salvation, then we must convince ourselves that she is even necessary for our eternal salvation. This has been taught by the great Saints and Doctors of the Church, from St. Ephrem to St. Cyril of Alexandria down to St. John Damascene, continuing on to St. Bernard, St. Alphonsus Liguori right up to St. Maximilian M. Kolbe. This means that the common doctrine of the Catholic Church regards devotion to Our Lady as something morally necessary for the Christian, both because the Mother holds a life-supporting role, and because we cannot succeed in conforming to Jesus, the Son of God and Son of Mary, unless we are tender and devoted sons of the common Mother of the whole Mystical Body. The more we are sons of Mary, the more we are brothers of Jesus; and vice versa.

Filial love

For us to be children of Mary also; to behave as children of Mary; to live and love Our Lady as children: It is not possible to give Mary an offering of oneself which would have more beauty, more depth, and more love than this. True devotion to Our Lady, as distinguished from devotion toward any other saint, is the devotion of true and proper children for their divine Mother. It is filial love. And we can say that all the Marian devotion of the saints has had its particular expression of intense filial love for her as their "dearest Mother" (St. Maximilian Kolbe), "good Mother" (St. Margaret M. Alacoque), "precious Mother" (St. Veronica Giuliani), "beautiful Mother" (St. Bertilla), "beloved Mother" (St. Alphonsus Liguori), in a word "my Mamma"[1] (St. Paul of the Cross, St. Gemma and many others).

But who can report all the tender utterances of the Saints' filial love for their heavenly Mother? The mere name of Mary "increased the heartbeats" of St. Thérèse

---

1 *Translator's note:* Literally 'mommy,' which reverently conveys what in English would be "fond Mother," or "dear Mother."

of Lisieux, caused St. Joseph of Cupertino to levitate in ecstasy, and brought tears of tender devotion to the eyes of St. Pio of Pietrelcina. And St. Vincent Pallotti, St. Bernadette, St. Gabriel of the Sorrowful Mother — how many fond kisses did they not give to Mary's images? With fervent kisses St. Stephen Bellesini wore out many images of Mary. St. Louis de Montfort and St. Joseph Cottolengo wished to be buried under Mary's altar. The holy Curé of Ars ventured to say, "If I were able, I would gladly sell myself in order to give something to Our Lady." St. Maximilian M. Kolbe experienced within himself such vehement love that he defined himself as the "fool for the Immaculate."

We may venture to say that the following strong sentiment of St. Bonaventure belongs to all the saints: "To say to you that you are my Mother is next to nothing; oh Mary, you are my absolute love!" Let us remember, too, the tender *Visits to the Blessed Virgin Mary* of St. Alphonsus Liguori; visits by which he has nourished the love of generations of devout souls and in which are contained the most precious and tender utterances of many saints towards our most sweet Mother. A reading of those *Visits* should deeply move us and make us mindful of our hardness of heart.

The first thing we must ask of Our Lady is precisely this: filial love. And we ought to beg for it with persistence, with humble and affectionate determination. In this regard, we ought to imitate St. Felix of Cantalice who was so attentive to being a good son of Mary that for forty years he always made this prayer when passing before a Marian shrine or altar: "O noble Mother of God, I desire to love you like a good son…"

Love opposed to sin

It is evident that one cannot love a person whom one is offending. This is above all true if the person is our heavenly Mother.

To her devoted children Our Lady can address these same words of Jesus: *"Abide in my love… You are my friends, if you do the things that I command you"* (Jn 15:9, 14). And what does Our Lady command us? At the marriage feast of Cana she said to the waiters, *"Whatever He shall say to you, do ye"* (Jn 2:5). Be faithful to Jesus and carry out His will in everything. This is what Mary asks. Sin is exactly the contrary. It is always rebellion nourished by selfishness and pride. Now Jesus has said, *"He that is not with Me is against Me"* (Mt 12:30). By sin we become Jesus' enemies. How, then, would it be possible to love Our Lady if one is Jesus' enemy? It is absurd.

St. Pius X advises us, "Everyone ought to be persuaded that if the devotion which he claims to have for the Blessed Virgin does not restrain him from sin or inspire in him a determination to live a better life, it is an artificial, false devotion, as it lacks its natural fruit."

"Who has true devotion to Mary?" asked St. Leonard of Port Maurice. And he answers, "He who is an enemy of sin."

In a beautiful sermon to the people, St. Joseph Cafasso explained this point. "Most of all I urge you not to displease Our Lady," he said. "Now there is only one thing that displeases her — sin. If a good son or good daughter knows that something causes his mother displeasure, he does not do it, for he reasons thus: 'I know that my mother does not look with favor on this; I know it offends her; I know it causes her displeasure; I know it disgusts her. Therefore I will not do it. I do not want it said that she suffers this displeasure from me...' My dear people, I would like for us to proceed in this way when we find ourselves in danger of committing a sin, of doing something that is not upright. Let us on that occasion say to ourselves, 'I know that this causes displeasure to Our Lady. I know that Blessed Mary does not look with favor on this. I know it disgusts her, that it offends her. Therefore I will not do it. I would not do it for all the gold in the world. No, Mary. I do not want to do you wrong. I am not willing to cause you this displeasure.'"

Defending our Mother

A special chapter on filial love for Our Lady tells the struggle undertaken by her sons to defend their Mother from attacks by heretics, by indifferent Christians, and by those who want to reduce the love and glory with which the holy Virgin should be honored.

St. Cyril was victorious in defending the Divine Maternity of Our Lady. St. Jerome vigorously fought errors that denied Mary's perpetual Virginity. St. John Damascene strongly defended the honor due the images of Mary, paying the price of having his hand cut off. St. Bernard caused Marian devotion to thrive when it was dwindling almost everywhere. St. Anthony defended and explained well the truth of Mary's Assumption. Bl. John Duns Scotus presented enlightening explanations of the privilege of the Immaculate Conception. In his celebrated *True Devotion to Mary*, St. Louis Grignion de Montfort vigorously and fervently upheld the excellence of devotion to Mary. St. Alphonsus Liguori fought the battle on every front in his *Glories of Mary*, upholding Mary's Immaculate Conception, her rank as Mediatrix of all graces, her Assumption into Heaven, and her Queenship. It is touching to learn how St. Alphonsus would shed tears in his fervor when he was writing against Our Lady's enemies. He was defending his Mother.

In our own day—against wild criticism so radical as to call for abolishing devotion to Our Lady—St. Maximilian M. Kolbe set forth the value of consecrating ourselves to Mary in an even more radical, complete way. He also upheld Mary's role as Mediatrix of all graces, and desired to see a solemn dogmatic declaration of this by the Church.

Against recent attacks on the Rosary, St. Pio of Pietrelcina defended the perennial worthiness of this prayer by the weight of his prestigious example; he recited his beads (five decades) more than a hundred times a day.

We, indeed, like all the saints, should earnestly seek to make our own two maxims of the great St. Bonaventure. The first is, "One should carefully beware of decreasing, even the slightest, the honor that is owed to Mary." And the second, "One should be ready to defend Mary's privileges even at the risk of his life." There have been many saints (for example, St. Leonard of Port Maurice, St. Alphonsus Liguori) who took the "vow even to shed their blood," if need be, in order to defend Mary's Immaculate Conception. In defense of their heavenly Mother, the love of true sons ventures even to death; for *charity never falleth away* (I Cor 13: 8).

BEING JESUS FOR MARY

If we are to love Our Lady as sons and daughters, we have a very holy Model to copy; and that is Jesus, Mary's Son, our divine Brother.

The greatest disciples of Mary are those who resemble Jesus the most in being Mary's own, as He was, and in loving her like a son, as He did. It is these who reach the point of *being Jesus for Mary.* In this way the highest kind of devotion to Mary is found only in one who has become transformed and identified with Jesus, whereby he can truthfully repeat with St. Paul, *"I live now not with my own life, but with the life of Christ who lives in me"* (Gal 2:20).

It cannot be otherwise. To grow in the spiritual life means to make *the old man* — which is our selfishness — die within us, in order for Jesus to live there, who is *the new man*, by our adopting His sentiments, His way of love in our thoughts, words, affections, desires, and deeds (cf. Eph 4:22; Col 3:9).

The selfsame love of Jesus for His divine Mother thus becomes also the love of one who has reached this identification with Jesus, and this is so in the measure of one's conformity with Him. When a person is interiorly "one" with Jesus, he is also "one" with Jesus in loving Our Lady; although no one, not even all creatures together, could ever exhaust the infinite magnitude of Jesus' love for His Mother. It is something that will delight us forever in Paradise.

Never too much

If our model in loving Our Lady is Jesus, one can well understand how completely out of place the worry is today of those people who see a risk here — the risk of loving Our Lady too much. It is literally true that this risk is non-existent.[2] No matter how far we might be likely to go in our happy enthusiasm and ingenuous follies of devotion, our love will be dwarfed beside the divine love that Jesus bore His Mother. Regrettably, we can never equal the measure of Jesus' love for His holy Mother. St. Maximilian M. Kolbe presented this sound advice: "Do not fear loving Our Lady too much; for you will never come to love her as Jesus loved her." And centuries earlier St. Bernard said that we will never succeed in "sufficiently" offering the praise and love due to God's Mother. "No one can ever be

---

2 *Translator's note:* Obviously we are speaking here of a well-ordered love for God's Mother as He desires it. God is the only object we love for his own sake and we love Mary and creatures in God and for God, to satisfy God's wish that we do so. In fact Mary refuses to accept any other kind of love and could not have been pleased with the cult of the Fourth Century Collyridians, who held that the holy Virgin was a divinity to whom must be offered sacrifices of adoration. This cult was vigorously combated in the writings of that great lover of Mary, St. Epiphanius, who called it idolatry and declared that "Mary, although perfect, was only a simple creature and could not be honored as God with their sacrifices" (cf. St. Alphonsus Liguori, *History of Heresies*, ch. 4, n. 78).

too devoted to the Blessed Virgin," St. Bonaventure adds in a fervent text.

Let us, then, hear out St. Alphonsus who writes the following with his usual persuasive grace: "When an opinion is of such a nature that it in some measure contributes more to the glory of the holy Virgin and one finds worthy grounds and insights in it that are not out of harmony with faith or with decrees of the Church or with truth, then refusal to accept it surely indicates little devotion to the Mother of God. Then it would be worse to attack it by the pretext: Who knows but that the contrary may be true? For my part I would not want to be one of those over-reluctant souls and I would not wish that my readers be of their mind. Let us rather be among those who fully and firmly believe whatever can be admissibly, reliably, accepted for Mary's glory without error. This full, uncomplicated believing in all her grandeurs is one of the most acceptable tributes that the Mother of God can receive from us."

Let us make the zeal of the Saints our own, their striving for utmost love which ventures beyond any mere measure and is in keeping with this exclamation of the Servant of God, Fr. Anselm Treves: "Would that I had billions of lives in order to live them all at the feet of Mary, billions of hearts in order to love her mightily."

But who will make us become another "Jesus for Mary"? The one who will do it is only Mary. For she alone is the "mold of Jesus," and only he who submits himself to this mold becomes *"conformed to Jesus"* (cf. Rom 8:29). Only in her, therefore, will we become her sons after the likeness of Jesus.

In little things

If we are poor and little in the spiritual life, and if our devotion is very little, then let us endeavor to *be Jesus for Mary* at least in the little things, in the many easy and simple opportunities that arise. Let us try, for example, to *be Jesus for Mary* at prayer each morning and each night, never failing to greet our Mother at the start and close of each day. We should strive to *be Jesus for Mary* by avoiding any word or deed that would be disrespectful to Our Lady, and we should cultivate respect and affection instead, with the practice of devout ejaculatory prayer to her.

St. Stanislaus Kostka lived his devotion to Our Lady very earnestly. He always invoked her before every undertaking and, when feasible, would turn in the direction of a church or toward a place where an image of Mary was venerated, in order to seem closer to her as he called on her.

St. Maximilian recommends: "During little sufferings, pray by making the invocation, 'Mary!' and tell her you want it all to serve whatever intentions are most acceptable to her. Thus you put your sufferings like a chisel into the hand of a master sculptor."

Once two confreres asked St. Pio of Pietrelcina if Our Lady was present in his cell during the bodily scourgings which he frequently underwent.[3] Padre Pio replied, "Ask me rather if Our Lady is ever absent from this cell!" Padre Pio was truly another Jesus for Mary, and she made him more so with every scourging which made him all the more like Jesus scourged.

Regarding the Servant of God Don Edward Poppe, we know that he, too, sought little occasions to conduct himself like another Jesus toward His Mother. For example, each morning as soon as he arose he used to kneel at Our Lady's feet to receive her blessing. There were times when he would pause so that she might go first when going in or out of a door; other times he would offer her holy water; and then there were the occasions when he would leave an empty seat near him where she might sit. There was even a time when he obtained an extra ticket for her to accompany him when he was traveling! These are little things, and they might seem a bit childish, but what earnest love they reveal!

Ah! If we could at least imagine Jesus' union with Our Lady, the great love with which He surrounded

3 *Translator's note:* By divine intervention Padre Pio was afflicted by both the stigmata, or Five Wounds of Christ, and also by suffering Christ's bloody scourging, which would leave his undershirt bathed in blood; for God sometimes grants remarkable sufferings to generous, well-disposed souls, for their greater merit and reward (Job 2:6; Gal 6:17; II Cor 12:7). This added immense fruitfulness to his labor to convert sinners; for thus he could *"fill in what was wanting in the sufferings of Christ"* (Col 1:24) to earn graces for countless conversions.

her, the tenderness with which He stood by her! If we could but picture how attentively He used to listen to her, how carefully He would obey her, and how gladly He would honor her!

Of St. Maximilian M. Kolbe, authors could say "that he breathed Mary. He had her name on his lips always — during work, when walking, in his conversations. When he used to pronounce 'Mary,' he seemed to breathe more deeply." If this is true of St. Maximilian, what must have been the case with Jesus?

We, too, ought to imitate Jesus. Grand things are not necessary in order to express our devotion to Mary, because the greatest of them is precisely the practice of pleasing our sweet Mother in all the little things of every day. This should be the ordinary fabric of our devotional life, woven together thread by thread, action by action, performed lovingly and out of affection for Our Lady. Let us ask Jesus for His own filial love, for if we have this, we will day by day acquire a likeness to Him and can truly be said to *be Jesus for Mary*, to the point of a perfect fulfillment of Jesus' words to Our Lady, *"Behold thy son"* (Jn 19:27).

In the Eucharistic Jesus

A very beautiful act which helps us to be *Jesus for Mary* in a very special way is Holy Communion. In those moments there is a physical union with Jesus as He is present in the one who has received Him. If the creature lets itself be completely possessed by Jesus so that Jesus might, in turn, let the creature completely possess Him, then Jesus and the creature are no longer two, but *one*. And we cannot give greater joy to Our Lady, according to St. Hilary, than by enabling her to see the Eucharistic Jesus present in us while we suitably keep Him company. Let us reflect: Every day we should be able to give this unspeakable joy to Our Lady. Every day we should be able to *be Jesus for Mary* in the most sublime way possible in this world, during those ten or fifteen minutes following Holy Communion — as long as the presence of the Sacred Host remains in our body. It would be a beautiful and fitting thing during those moments to renew our consecration to Our Lady by singing the *Magnificat* with her and with the Angels, as Bl. Contardo Ferrini used to do.

And what shall we say of spiritual Communions? These would keep us united to the Eucharistic Jesus by continually giving us His Heart in order to love Our Lady with His throbbing love. Hence, St. Maximilian, among his resolutions, pledged himself to make a spiritual Communion *every quarter of an hour*. This is the behavior of great lovers of Mary!

During visits to the Blessed Sacrament we do well to recall that there is no place on earth where Our Lady is more present than where any tabernacle contains the Holy Eucharist. St. Mary Victoria Teresa Coudere left her religious Sisters the practice of the *contemplation of Mary in the Cenacle* as a special means of perfection. The incomparable Apostle of the Eucharist, St. Peter

Julian Eymard, used to say that "to become good servants of the Eucharist it is necessary to be docile and devoted sons of Mary," and he liked to call the Blessed Virgin Mary "Our Lady of the Blessed Sacrament." St. Pio of Pietrelcina used to ask his flock, "Don't you, too, see Our Lady near the altar?" When a spiritual daughter asked him if Our Lady assisted at his Mass, Padre Pio promptly queried, "Do you think the Mother is not concerned with her son?" For this reason St. Alphonsus always put his *Visits to the Blessed Sacrament* together with his *Visits to the Blessed Virgin Mary*. And St. Maximilian desired that every altar of the Blessed Sacrament be surmounted by an image of the Immaculate, because Jesus and Mary are but *one* and we aspire to become *one* with Them. Where the Son is, there is the Mother. Where the Mother is, there is the Son.

BEING MARY FOR JESUS

The final aim of devotion to Our Lady is not Our Lady, but Jesus. Yes, it is Jesus.

True devotion to Our Lady is not an end in itself, but it is a means of love, a way of love, an effort of love which brings me to the final goal of my existence, namely, Jesus and His Paradise.

Jesus is the Beginning and the End of all things (cf. Apoc 21:6). All things were made by Him (cf. Jn 1:3), including the Blessed Virgin — in fact, she, above all. Without Jesus, Our Lady would never have existed.

To love Our Lady, to consecrate oneself to her and belong to her without reserve means, then, to give oneself to her who is wholly directed to Jesus, to her who has been given to Jesus for an everlasting role, and who gives herself to Jesus with all those who are entrusted to her. The path of Marian devotion proceeds to Jesus with Mary and in Mary. St. Louis Grignion de Montfort rightly declares: Devotion to Our Lady consists essentially "in the gift of one's entire self to Mary, and by means of her, to Jesus, and then, in doing everything with Mary, in Mary, and through Mary."

All clients of Our Lady ought to realize the inspired words of St. Ambrose: "May Mary's soul be within you to magnify God. May Mary's spirit be within you to rejoice in the Lord."

Entering within the "Palace"

St. Maximilian M. Kolbe used to say that Our Lady is like a wonderful palace. Far within and at the center, Jesus rules as King. To go to Jesus, therefore, we must enter into this palace. "Hail, His Palace!" exclaimed St. Francis of Assisi.

It is, therefore, necessary to enter into Mary. That is, we must love Mary so much as to unite ourselves with her, pass into her, and enclose ourselves within her. Transformation of oneself into her: this is how St. Louis Grignion and St. Maximilian M. Kolbe express it. St. Maximilian adopts the daring and telling expression to "transubstantiate oneself" into Mary, in order "to become her, so that she alone remains in us." The Servant of God Charles De Foucauld said that he also wished "to become another Mary, alive and active," to be "marianized", that is to say, realizing in Mary the celebrated words of St. Paul: *"For me to live is Mary,"* and *"I live now not with my own life, but with the life of Mary, who lives in me."* (cf. Phil 1:21; Gal 2:20). But why all this?

Because to become Mary means managing to love Jesus by participating in that noble way of life realized in the most exalted of creatures; it means managing to please Jesus, to gladden and delight Him, by letting Him see in us the heavenly profile of His Blessed Mother, letting Him perceive in our hearts the movements of the pure and fragrant love that His ever-Virgin Mother had.

St. Maximilian M. Kolbe teaches that if we keep growing in devotion to Our Lady, we reach a point where "she loves her Divine Son with our poor hearts. We become a means through which the Immaculate loves Jesus; and Jesus, seeing us as her possession and, as it were, a part and parcel of our holy Mother, loves her in us and through us."

Hence, true devotion to Mary, far from depriving Jesus of anything, is for Jesus the sweetest joy; it is the most delightful happiness brought to His filial Heart. One day St. Gertrude heard a sermon in which Our Lady was devoutly praised while nothing was said about Jesus. The Saint regretted the silence about Jesus; and as she passed an image of Mary, she felt little fervor as she paid Our Lady her usual reverence. Jesus suddenly appeared to her and said, "Every tribute made to My Mother, I regard as made to Me." The Son cannot be offended or displeased if He sees His Mother honored and loved. Rather, the contrary is true.

The great St. Bernard declared, "Nothing delights me so much as to speak of the glories of the Virgin Mother." The humble St. Bernadette Soubirous used to say she had only one fond ambition, that of seeing Our Lady "loved and glorified" by all. St. Jane de Chantal wrote that "prayer is made according to a method very pleasing to the holy Virgin when God is praised for the great things He has done in her and for the choice He made of her to be His worthy and true Mother."

Thus, the Church has always taught that union with Our Lady not only "does not in the least hinder close contact with Christ, but it even facilitates it" (*Lumen Gentium*, 60). It cannot be otherwise; for the more one is united to Mary, the more he is united to Jesus.

The best road

It is noteworthy that true and perfect devotion to Mary brings us Jesus, our one Goal, by the best road, the road that is most glorious, the road chosen and traveled by Himself to come to us. St. Bernard calls Mary "the royal road of the Savior." Now if Jesus chose this road as His way to give Himself to us, should we ever expect to find another better road as a means of giving ourselves to Him? God's way of acting is one of perfection. If we act differently, we necessarily fall into imperfection.

On this point, St. Louis Grignion and St. Maximilian both declare that perfect devotion to Mary is "the road that is easy, short, perfect, and sure, for reaching union with Our Lord"; for Our Lady has the motherly skill to make harsh things mild, to make bitter things sweet, and to soften what is too hard. Bl. Contardo Ferrini used to say, "If the way that leads to Jesus' Heart is arduous and long, have one look at the Heart of this Mother, and you will have courage!"

Yes, Our Lady truly makes distances shorter, makes traveling better, and enables us to get there sooner.

Once St. Pio of Pietrelcina was asked by one of his spiritual sons, "Father, teach me a short cut to reach God." Padre Pio answered, "The shortcut is the Virgin."

Now if devotion to Our Lady is indeed the *shortcut* to holiness, why risk any longer routes? We ought rather to thank God for making available to us this heavenly *shortcut* which we can call the *express route* to the Heart of Jesus. With characteristic, wholesome fervor, St. Alphonsus Liguori encourages us to strive toward the highest goals, and exhorts us to ask Our Lady to give us a quick passage thither in her arms: "Ah, my Lady! If you do not carry me in your arms to God, do not expect me to walk there. Carry me, and if I resist, carry me by force."

The white ladder

Devotion to Mary is that *white ladder* seen by Brother Leo in a celebrated vision. In this vision the holy friar saw an immense field, and in it there were so many friars of the Order that to get them all within view the throng had to extend upward even to Heaven. Two ladders also appeared there rising into the sky, one of them red and one of them white. At the top of the red one St. Francis was seen alongside Jesus, and he invited the friars to mount up. The friars faithfully undertook the climb, but afterwards fell back down, some from the first rung, others from the second rung, and others fell from the third. Even the few who seemed to reach the top rung with great labor — even fell back down. Then the Seraphic Father encouraged his sons, "Have confidence! Have confidence! Hasten over there to the white ladder." And there, in all her beauty, the Immaculate Virgin was inviting her protégés to climb up to her. Then — how wonderful to see it! — they all climbed the white ladder with agility, all the way to the top.

It is all-important to realize that true devotion to Our Lady is the most perfect way to Jesus — the noblest and the most beautiful way.

Has there ever been another creature like Our Lady, so united to Jesus, belonging so totally to Jesus, living so fully with Jesus and for Jesus? Not one creature! — neither in Heaven nor on earth!

To *be Mary for Jesus* means, then, to offer Him the gift of oneself in the most precious, the sweetest, the most gentle way. It is behaving humbly toward Jesus, treating Him with love, surrounding Him with respectful and awed affection and tender fondness — just as Our Lady did. What an ideal for us poor mortals to achieve! And yet, perfect devotion to Our Lady brings us to a transformation into Mary, makes us become her *"image and likeness"* (cf. Gen 1:26), in order to please Jesus.

Perhaps we can now understand better why St. John Berchmans used to say, "I will give myself no peace until I have true devotion to Our Lady." Hence, we can understand better why all the saints fondly and eagerly cultivated devotion to Our Lady, and why, in their prayers, they pleaded that they would succeed in this, as St. Maximilian recommended we do.

"I have never read of any Saint," declares St. Bonaventure, "who did not have a special devotion to the glorious Virgin." Here we have the truth. And what is more, that heavenly zeal to outdo everyone in loving for Our Lady is mesmerizing in the Saints. This was the spirit of St. John Eudes, who could not be resigned to the idea that anyone might succeed in loving Our Lady more than he; or the spirit of St. Teresa of Jesus when she wrote that her ardent aim was: "I want to be, after Jesus, the person who has loved Our Lady most."

"He that honoreth his mother is as one that layeth up a treasure."

(Ec 3:5)

Chapter II

WHY DEVOTION TO OUR LADY?

- ◆ **Our Lady is our fond Mother**

- ◆ **Our Lady is Immaculate**

- ◆ **Our Lady is Queen**

- ◆ **Our Lady is Mediatrix**

- ◆ **Our Lady is the "Gate of Heaven"**

OUR LADY IS OUR FOND MOTHER

We ought to be devoted to Our Lady because she is our fond Mother.

Once when St. John Bosco was giving an instruction, he asked his audience, "Who is Our Lady?" He received various replies — "Our Lady is Mother of God... She is Queen of Heaven... She is the Immaculate Virgin..." But there was one answer that the Saint wanted above all. He gave it himself: "Our Lady is our fond Mother."

Yes, the Mother of God, the Queen of Heaven, the Immaculate, the Virgin Assumed into Paradise is our own Mother.

Our Lady is the divinely appointed Mother of the Mystical Body; she is the Mother of Jesus and of us who are Jesus' brethren. Pope Paul VI declared, "Our Lady is Christ's Mother, and hence the Mother of God and our Mother."

Behold thy Mother

The first foundation for devotion to Our Lady is her status as Mother and our status as her children. The divine words of Jesus to Mary, *"Behold, thy son,"* and to His disciple John, *"Behold thy Mother"* (Jn 19:27) have to do with each one of us.

In considering such a reality, sentiments of love and tenderness ought to strongly move us: the very Motherhood which Our Lady had towards Jesus extends to each one of us, and she takes us all as her children in a spiritual way within her bosom, her Heart, her arms.

Thanks be to God the Father, to God the Son, to God the Holy Spirit!

Once a query about Our Lady brought this worthy response from Padre Pio, "Our Lady is our Mother." And he could not restrain from being moved even to tears. What truth could be sweeter for us?

We should thus appreciate the sentiment of St. Maximilian M. Kolbe when along the streets of Rome he heard a man blaspheme Our Lady. He left his companions, went over to the man, and with tears in his eyes said, "You would blaspheme her, your Mother?" Impressed by the young friar, the man asked pardon and promised not to do it again.

When we realize that Our Lady is our fond Mother, when we hear it said, when we say it ourselves, we ought to experience joy.

Consider the devotion with which St. Gemma Galgani called Our Lady "Mamma!" She seemed never to weary addressing Mary in this way. In one of her ecstasies she called Our Lady "Mamma" some thirty times. Once she opened her heart to Our Lady thus: "O my Mamma! What a joy it is to call you Mamma! You see how my heart exults, just as it does when I think of Jesus."

Beside our cradle

When is it that Our Lady becomes our Mother, and we her children?

It is in holy Baptism. With the reception of baptismal grace into the soul we are born again *"in water and in the Holy Spirit"* (Jn 3:5), becoming children of God and of Mary and brethren of Jesus.

St. Leo the Great had good grounds for his statement that every baptismal font is where the holy Virgin becomes a Mother. We ought to conclude from this that every Christian emerges from his re-birth in Baptism as a devotee of Our Lady, for he is then born a child of Mary, and a child's devotion towards his mother is instinctive. Together with the natural mother, watching beside every baptized child's cradle, there stands the heavenly Mother. While the natural mother is a true mother, the heavenly Mother, Mary, is even more so, because Mary is the Mother of the spiritual life, whereas the natural mother brought forth only the life of the body. Our Lady is as much more of a real Mother to us as the supernatural order surpasses the natural. Thus Saints like St. Joseph of Cupertino rightly considered our earthly mother to be a mere "nurse", in comparison to the Mother of our spiritual life. St. Cajetan's mother consecrated him to Our Lady from his birth and regarded herself as only the boy's "nurse"; and she used to call him "Mary's Cajetan."

It is certainly a sweet and blessed practice to consecrate one's little children to Our Lady, who is the true Mother of us all. There have been Christian mothers who had the holy inspiration to consecrate their little ones to Our Lady even before they were born. The mothers of St. Anthony of Padua and St. Peter M. Chanel, for example, did this.

Bl. Stephen Bellesini, who was parish priest for many years at the Marian Sanctuary in Genazzano, introduced the pious practice of taking infants immediately after their baptism to Our Lady's altar to consecrate them to the heavenly Mother. The holy Curé of Ars urged all parents to consecrate their children daily to Our Lady, as the Mother of St. Gerard used to do. Let mothers and fathers be mindful of these examples and be disposed to imitate them.

She loves us beyond compare

Faith alone enables us to perceive these truths — a faith which sheds light upon the most profound, delightful, and vital contents of our relationship with Our Lady. We are inseparably bound to her as a son has ties to his mother. And we, as her children, are bound to her not with ties of *"flesh and blood"* (Jn 1:18), but with ties of the Spirit, with loftier and more indestructible ties. No comparison is possible between the love our heavenly Mother bears us and that of any other mother. The holy Curé of Ars wisely declared, "Mary's Heart is so loving toward us that the hearts of all other mothers taken together are but a piece of ice in comparison... The holy Virgin is so kind that she always treats us affectionately and never punishes us. The Son wields His justice, while the Mother has nothing but love."

Once St. Alphonsus Rodriguez broke out into ardent exclamations when he was praying to Our Lady: "How much you mean to me, O Queen of the Angels and Mother of my God! … How great is the love I bear you! … It is greater than the love you have for me!…" Our Lady then appeared to him in great beauty and sweetness and affectionately answered, "No, Alphonsus; that is not so. You are deceiving yourself: much greater is the love I have for you, beyond comparison." The same Saint, when he became an old man, while climbing a mountain to pray in a chapel dedicated to Our Lady, felt a light hand wipe the perspiration that streamed down his forehead. Note how far Our Lady's motherly devotedness can go!

We have matter for reflection on Our Lady's loving kindness that concerns itself with even simple things like household chores. Once St. Catherine of Siena was seen being helped by Our Lady in making bread. When St. Zita was lost one night, Our Lady was seen escorting her back home. St. Veronica Giuliani was assisted by Our Lady when doing the laundry. Thus it came about that the Saint became much faster in doing her washing than her religious sisters, and those sisters realized that Our Lady was helping her; for now and then St. Veronica would speak as though it were to someone else, "O my

Madonna, do you want to do it all yourself? Do you want me to do nothing at all?"

Thus Bl. Contardo Ferrini was not going to any excess when he used to end his letters by urging his correspondent to remember him in prayer "to our most loving and dear Mother." Likewise the Saints were not exaggerating when they gave her titles describing her unlimited tender love.

St. Pio of Pietrelcina, in a letter to his spiritual Father, even ventures to call Our Lady a "tyrant" because of the "wonderful and great graces" which she poured into his heart in such abundance that he could take no more and became "exasperated." What sweet tyranny and what happy exasperation! One can rightly say of Our Lady's love what St. Paul said of Jesus' love, that it *surpasseth all knowledge*" (Eph 3:19).

You never go too far in loving her

Our Lady is God's masterpiece of love, of every love God has instilled in creatures — motherly love, filial love, spousal love, virginal love. St. Maximilian M. Kolbe ventured to say that the Immaculate is the quasi-incarnation of the Holy Spirit who is Love: she is the created Immaculate Conception, whereas the Holy Spirit is the Uncreated Immaculate Conception.

Let us be eager, then, to return her love, even if we can never love her as much as we ought. Once a spiritual daughter said to St. Pio, "You are fortunate, Father, to love Our Lady so much." Padre Pio answered, "I wish I could love her as much as she deserves. But remember that all the Saints and Angels together cannot love and praise the Mother of God according to her worth."

We must never feel we go too far in loving Our Lady. *"They that eat me shall yet hunger: and they that drink me shall yet thirst"* (Ec 24:29). The Liturgy puts that text on the lips of the Blessed Virgin. Great and holy souls have loved her so much that they could not help wanting to die quickly in order to be with her. Saints expressing themselves this way have been, for example, St. Stanislaus Kostka, St. Anthony M. Claret, and St. Bernadette Soubirous.

Once some fellow friars sent St. Maximilian Kolbe their good wishes that he might soon go to Heaven to be with the Immaculate. The Saint answered, "I especially thank those who… did not wish me a long life, but an early death, so that I may be with the Immaculate."

The zealous apostle St. Leonard of Port Maurice, used to tell people, even from the pulpit, of his wish to die quickly in order to join the Blessed Virgin in Paradise. Once, when preaching, he ventured to say "I strongly wish to die in order to live with Mary. Recite a Hail Mary for me. Obtain the grace for me to die now in this pulpit. I want to go see Mary." His desire for Mary was like the vehement craving that burned in St. Paul's heart for Christ, so that he could say: *"I … having a desire to be dissolved and to be with Mary"* (cf. Phil 1:23).

One who loves, does not think in the same way as one who does not love.

The deathbed

If Our Lady was watching over us when we were newly born in Baptism, we ought to greatly desire that she be at our bedside at our last hour. Do we not ask this in every Hail Mary? — "Pray for us sinners, now and at the hour of our death." It is on our deathbed that the final battle which determines our eternal fate is fought. If we have Our Lady with us, we can be sure that then, as always, *"she will crush the head"* of the infernal serpent (Gen 3:15).

For this reason, the Saints' practice has been to pray and hope that they would have Our Lady at hand at the hour of death. Note these touching words of St. Alphonsus in his Visits to the Blessed Virgin: "O Mary, my Mother, for the love you have for God I beg you to help me always, but especially during the last hours of my life. Do not leave me until you see me safe in Heaven, blessing and singing your mercies for all eternity. This I hope for. May it come to be!"

St. Bonaventure wrote that "devoutly invoking the Virgin is a sign of salvation." A final prayer to Mary accompanied the passage of many Saints into the life hereafter. Nor can we forget that Jesus seems to have said *"Mother!"* in the cry He uttered on the Cross before expiring (cf. Mt 27:50 and Mk 15:37) — a final, fond gesture of the sacred Humanity of the Son toward

His sweet Mother. But let us consider the examples of some of the saints.

St. Francis of Assisi died at the friary of St. Mary of the Angels at the feet of the heavenly Queen.

St. Anthony of Padua died singing the Marian hymn *O gloriosa Domina! Excelsa super sidera…* (O glorious Lady, exalted above the stars).

On his deathbed St. Camillus de Lellis wanted a picture of Christ crucified with Our Lady at the foot of the Cross. With what earnest he begged the Sorrowful Virgin to intercede for him!

St. Joseph Benedict Labre died after a final, lengthy prayer before Our Lady of the Mountains in Rome.

St. John Joseph of the Cross was pronouncing his last words during his final agony when he said to a confrere, "Be mindful of Our Lady!"

Bl. Anna M. Taigi died while exhorting her family to have devotion to Our Lady and to recite the Rosary every day.

St. Bernadette died as she prayed, "Holy Mary, pray for me, a poor sinner…"

During his last agony St. Gabriel of Our Lady of Sorrows appeared restless. It was judged that he wanted to change his position. "No," he whispered, "the image of Our Lady." It was on his bed, but between the folds of the covers. They gave it to him. He looked at it with deep affection and said, "O my Mother, hurry!"

St. Vincent Gerosa, before expiring, said this final word, "Mary!"

Bl. Agostina Pierantoni and St. Bertilla Boscardin died with this final prayer on their lips, "My Lady, help me!"

A few days before her death St. Gemma Galgani wrote a letter to Our Lady. At a certain point, addressing Jesus, she said, "Take my poor soul, O Jesus. Entrust it to Your Mother, and I shall not be afraid, even of hell." Just before she expired she said, "My Mother, I entrust my soul to you. Tell Jesus to have mercy on me."

As St. Pio of Pietrelcina died, even up to his final inaudible breath he kept muttering the two names he loved, "Jesus — Mary."

There have been saints who received the favor of dying on a day specially dedicated to Our Lady. St. Rita of Cascia died on a Saturday in the month of May. St. John of the Cross likewise died on a Saturday. St. Jacinto and St. Stanislaus Kostka died on the Assumption. Bl. Magdalene de Canossa died on the feast of Our Lady of Sorrows. Bl. Stephen Bellesino requested and obtained the favor of dying with a lucid mind while praying the Rosary, and this was on February 2nd, the feast of Mary's Purification. St. Gemma Galgani died on Holy Saturday. St. Maximilian M. Kolbe died on August 14th at the time of First Vespers of the Assumption.

Other saints have had the privilege of dying during an ecstasy while having a vision of Our Lady, as St. John of God, Bl. Angelico, St. Gerard, St. Paul of the Cross. St. Antonino could make the beautiful statement on the day of his death, "Today I will see my Mother!" At the hour of his death, Our Lady said these consoling words to St. John of God for the benefit of all devout souls: "This is the hour in which I am accustomed never to be absent from my devoted servants."

We need not add that nearly all saints had the Rosary in their hands at that moment, as a visible tie with the Blessed Virgin — a kind of token of being taken by the hand into the next world by the heavenly Queen.

Happy is the death of one who is calling on Mary! In those supreme moments one's prayer to Our Lady draws down the heavenly comfort of feeling the presence of the Mother of all mercy. When one loves Our Lady, the recollection of that love gives him a filial confidence that he will be saved. St. Maddalena Sophia Barat in her pleasing way said, "The death of one truly devoted to Mary is a child's leap into his mother's arms."

After his death, St. Dominic Savio appeared in glory to St. John Bosco, who was overjoyed and wanted to ask a few questions:

"What was it that consoled you most at the point of death?" "Don Bosco, take a guess."

"Perhaps it was the thought of having preserved so well the flower of purity?"

"No."

"Was it the thought of the penances you performed during life?"

"Not even that."

"Then it may have been your peaceful conscience — being free from all sin?"

"That thought was a help to me. But what consoled me most at the hour of death was the thought that I had been devoted to Our Lady. Tell this to your young people and be insistent in your appeal for devotion to Our Lady."

This holy appeal is intended also for us.

OUR LADY IS IMMACULATE

Another basis of devotion to Our Lady is her Immaculate Conception.

Our Lady was created by God as the masterpiece of a new, redeemed humanity. She was created in grace as a model for the whole Church, which, "contemplating her hidden sanctity," sees in Mary what she, the Church, ought to become, and turns to Mary as the "exalted type" that is to be faithfully copied (*Lumen Gentium*, nn. 64–65).

The divine marvels contained in the Immaculate Conception make the Virgin Mary into the supremely great creature, beautiful beyond comparison, above all the choirs of Angels and inferior only to God.

St. Joseph of Cupertino — the Saint noted for remarkable levitations, when he was in the presence of an image of Mary — would often be dazzled by her splendor and, unable to restrain himself, would rise in a levitation, while he would ardently cry, "O lovely Mary! O lovely Mary!" Once when he was in the Basilica at Assisi with some other friars in the Chapel of the Immaculate, while gazing at the image of Mary he turned with an earnest expression to the Father Guardian who was nearby and said to him fervently, "Father Guardian, say with me, 'Lovely Mary! Lovely

Mary!'" The Father Guardian good-naturedly repeated the words, but without the great fervor of the Saint, who, with greater earnestness cried, "Father Guardian, say more loudly, 'Lovely Mary! Lovely Mary!'" The Guardian tried to repeat the words in a louder voice, but his attention was absorbed at seeing the Saint's face all aglow. The Saint impetuously clasped Father Guardian, almost embracing him, and in an ecstasy levitated off the floor, taking the Guardian with him toward the image of the "Lovely Mary."

Something similar happened to St. Ubaldo. One day while he was in the countryside singing the Litany of the Blessed Virgin, his body rose in an ecstatic levitation and rested upon a tree, as he exclaimed, "How beautiful you are, my dear Mother! How beautiful you are!"

On his deathbed Bl. Angelico appeared to be in ecstasy during his last moments. With his features aglow, he declared, "Our Lady is far lovelier than I have painted her to be!" Could it ever be otherwise? If the sacred Scriptures described Queen Esther as having *incredible beauty* (Es 2:15), what must we say of the Immaculate?

The Paradise of God

There will never be a suitable measure of admiration and praise paid to this Virgin conceived immaculate, this "Paradise of God," as St. Germain called her. The Carmelite mystic, St. Mary Magdalene de Pazzi, described Our Lady as "one giving full satisfaction to the Trinity." She added to this figure of speech that if — supposing the absurd — God were not in Paradise, Our Lady would be able to provide a Paradise for all the angels and saints.

This is no exaggeration. Sometimes it may happen to us that we feel unable to describe the wonderful beauties and grandeurs we see in something belonging to this world. What, then, must Our Lady be like? St. Bernadette declared that "once one sees Mary, he wants no more of this world."

One time Padre Pio spoke during an ecstasy and his spiritual director took down these words which he heard him say about Our Lady: "Ah, my lovely Mother! My dear Mother! ... You have such beautiful eyes! ... Jesus was right... Yes, you are beautiful... If faith did not teach us otherwise, men would call you a God... Your eyes shine with greater splendor than the sun... You are lovely, dear Mother. I am so glad of this, and love you..."

His ecstatic experience included the statement, "If faith did not teach us otherwise, men would call you a God." In the Immaculate Conception, as a matter of fact, we find a delightful and amazing likeness to the Divinity, because Immaculate Conception means fullness of Grace, fullness of divine Life, fullness of Love. *Grace, divine Life, Love* — these are almost personified in Our Lady: behold Mary Immaculate, the Daughter of the Eternal Father, Mother of the

Eternal Son, the Bride of the Eternal Spirit. The entire Holy Trinity bears this kinship to the Blessed Virgin, a kinship that is beyond words. She is that person who is "entirely divinized", as St. Peter Damian said. Hence St. Maximilian aptly said that the truth of the Immaculate Conception "is full of very consoling mysteries."

A creature both human and heavenly

Let us also consider how the Immaculate Conception constitutes the perfect example of a human person. Only the Immaculate is the creature at once fully human and fully heavenly; quite innocent, yet quite beautiful; pure, yet all sweetness; a Virgin full of refinement — a Virgin daughter, a Virgin Spouse, a Virgin Mother, a Virgin who is everlasting, all-powerful and most merciful, who is the Seat of wisdom, the noble Sovereign of love. The Immaculate Conception has been the fountainhead of all these wonders in Mary. For this reason, St. Paul of the Cross and St. Maximilian M. Kolbe thanked the Holy Trinity in every Mass for having created the Immaculate as one so great and so sublime. One would never reach the end in contemplating the Immaculate who is like a heaven spread out as an endless vault of sparkling stars. Every excellence that God and men could possibly imagine, long for, or dream of in a creature, has been included in Mary. St. Bernard aptly wrote: "O Mary, in all the world you are unique. You never had any model before you to pattern yourself by; and the world, even if it were to last forever, shall never have your equal." Once an album was shown to St. Bernadette containing the most famous works of art portraying Our Lady. As she turned through the pages, she remarked her dissatisfaction: "Why are people not ashamed to paint these strange things?"

In the Papal declaration defining the dogma of the Immaculate Conception, Pope Bl. Pius IX wrote that the Immaculate Conception "surpasses all praises given by heaven and earth… It is God's preeminent miracle — the height, indeed, of all miracles." And the Second Vatican Council upholds the teaching that Our Lady "far surpasses all other creatures, heavenly and earthly" (*Lumen Gentium*, n. 53). We now perhaps understand better why St. Maximilian could often repeat, "My Immaculate and my all, my all, my all!"

"You are all beautiful, O Mary!"

If Mary Immaculate is the matchless model of perfection in a human personality, then whoever wants to have a true, human personality that is most upright according to God, ought to look upon this supreme model in order to imitate her. It is useless to look elsewhere; for there does not exist on earth or in Heaven another human person who is perfect like the Immaculate. All the saints, even taken together, are inferior to the most Blessed Virgin. To turn to others and overlook her, means to overlook the most perfect model we could have. But if we follow her as our model, then our Marian devotion, besides promoting the glory of the Immaculate, will also help us to learn from her how best to develop our own personality as children of God. Thus elevated and strong, our personality will then blossom and flourish in the relentless fight against sin (the devil, the world, the flesh), in the triumph of grace (the serpent trampled under the feet of the Immaculate), in the fullness of love for God and neighbor, in purity of body and soul, in a humility that brings us to empty our self so that God can hold sway.

Such was the Immaculate. And it is in her that we see reflected the highest divine beauty in human vesture. It is this beauty of Mary which causes the entire Church to sing so frequently: "You are all fair, O Mary; in you there is no trace of original sin." How many times we are uplifted by such Marian music! What will it be like to see the Immaculate face to face? When St. Bernadette was asked if Our Lady was beautiful, the Saint answered, "She is so lovely that after seeing her once, one would want to die so that he could see her again."

An ancient writer of the Near East, George of Nicomedia, could say to Our Lady: "O loveliest beauty of all beauties!"

For women in particular, the Immaculate sets the wonderful example; for she is "the outstanding model of the condition of womanhood and the worthiest pattern for living by the Gospel" (Paul VI). In the

Immaculate every woman can find herself elevated and transfigured by grace according to God's plan of love, well understood by the men who were saints, who always endeavored to see Our Lady in every woman; as we know, for example, from resolutions made by Bl. Henry Suso, St. Gerard Majella, St. Gabriel of Our Lady of Sorrows.

The virgin, the wife, the mother, the daughter; the home-maker, the woman faced with the public; the woman responsible in making choices and reaching decisions, in undertaking affairs of great importance; the humble but strong woman, patient yet courageous, restrained but generous even to the point of total self-effacement: every woman, whatever her state of life, can find in the Immaculate, her own womanhood raised to purest perfection. She thus brings consolation and encouragement to our race, and gives a joy to the Heart of God as He gazes on His *all fair* masterpiece.

OUR LADY IS QUEEN

St. Thérèse of the Child Jesus called Our Lady "Queen of my heart." We, too, should have devotion to Our Lady because she is our Queen and because it is a duty of subjects to love, honor, and praise their Queen.

Our Lady has a share in the divine royalty of Jesus. She was Mother of the supreme King. One could say she was Jesus' Queen-Mother, and in Heaven takes her place now in glory at her Son's right hand: *"The queen stood on Thy right hand in gilded clothing"* (Ps 44:10).

Her status as God's Mother and her Immaculate Conception truly make Our Lady Queen of the universe, Empress of Paradise. It is she who can say to God, *"Thou art my Son"* (Ps 2:7). She can say to all Heaven and earth, *"The Lord possessed me in the beginning of His ways, before He made anything from the beginning. I was set up from eternity, and of old before the earth was made. The depths were not as yet, and I was already conceived: neither had the fountains of waters as yet sprung out. The mountains with their huge bulk had not as yet been established: before the hills were brought forth"* (Pr 8:22–25).[4]

---

4 *Translator's note*: As St. Bernardine of Siena explains, Mary was "preordained in God's mind before all creation" in order that she "might beget God as man" (Serm. 15, c. 4). Thus the world was created for the

The Woman clothed with the sun

If we were to seriously reflect upon this sublime reality of our Faith, we would find it a small thing that hosts of angels, according to the private revelations made to saints about the veneration paid to Our Lady during her earthly life, were ever at her side to respectfully and lovingly minister to her. We would have to say that these revelations give us a mere glimpse of the veneration and love that the holy angels must have really shown their Queen. St. Bridget, Ven. Katherine Emmerich, and Ven. Mary of Agreda have described something of what they learned in ecstasies and certain remarkable visions they had. The holy Fathers and Doctors of the Church have tried to explain in lofty figures the splendors of Mary's Queenship. "But she has been so exalted by God," says St. Maximilian M. Kolbe, "that all the tributes that the most loving souls will pay her till the end of the world will not measure up to the glory of which she is worthy."

Once St. Pio of Pietrelcina was on the veranda of his monastery with some other friars, and he heard some people singing a hymn to Our Lady with the refrain, "You are lovely as the sun, fairer than the moon". At these words Padre Pio said abruptly, "If Our Lady were only as those words say, I would refuse to go to Paradise." A confrere then asked, "Is Our Lady really

---

Immaculate Queen foreseen in God's mind; and she, in the fullness of time, was created for God.

that much more beautiful?" Padre Pio muttered, "Ah! More than you could ever imagine!"

Pope Pius XII, who solemnly proclaimed the feast of Mary's Queenship, left us some immortal pages on this consoling truth. He warmly urges us, "Maintain an earnest admiration for the Immaculate. Never be afraid that you might exalt her too much, she who will shine throughout eternity as God's masterpiece, as the most wonderful of His creatures, as the brightest mirror of the divine perfections."

But God Himself gives us the most glorious portrayal of Mary as Queen in the pages of Sacred Scripture, where the black gloom produced by Satan through our first parents' fall into original sin, is brightened by the prophecy of the *"Woman"* who, with her Son, would one day triumph over the infernal serpent and crush his head. This is the Queen triumphant over sin, the Queen of love and of glory whom the Prophet was to see going forth *"fair as the moon, bright as the sun, fearsome as an army set in battle array"* (Cant 6:9), and whom St. John the Evangelist was to see appearing in the heavens at the end of time *"clothed with the sun, and the moon under her feet, and on her head a crown of twelve stars"* (Apoc 12:1).

Her glory is our joy

The Queenship of Our Lady is a measureless glory for herself. It is a glory won by humility — a humility that was measureless. *"God exalteth the humble"* (Lk

1:52). St. Bonaventure asserts that God so exalted Our Lady for her humility, that now the creatures in Heaven, on earth, and in hell must kneel at her royal name, as they do at the name of Jesus. St. Augustine said the same, as well as St. Bernard, St. Louis de Montfort, and above all St. Alphonsus de Liguori.

But Mary's Queenship is also our joy. What a beautiful thing to have our Mother so highly glorified in Heaven, to have our Mother reigning as Queen in Paradise! How could a son fail to rejoice at the glory of his mother? What son would not want to see his mother honored?

St. Thérèse of the Child Jesus wrote a final note before her death that included this delightful and completely Marian thought: "O Mary, if I were Queen of Heaven and you were Thérèse, I would want to be Thérèse so that you might be Queen of Heaven!"

Therefore what a pitiful sight are all those people who do not love Our Lady as their Queen and even go so far as to labor to demote her from her royal rank by considering her as just an ordinary woman!

What kind of sons are these? They show their affections to be just the opposite of what they should be. Instead of bringing honor to their mother, they try to downgrade her, as though it were something shameful to honor her.

St. Pio of Pietrelcina once learned from some demons that when, in an attempt to trick souls, they disguise themselves to look like the Blessed Virgin

Mary, they pay for it more dearly than if they make themselves look like Jesus. Oh, how much God treasures the honor of His Mother! True sons take better care of their mother than of themselves. When St. Alphonsus Liguori wrote his wonderful book *The Glories of Mary*, he chose to dedicate it to Jesus. Why? Because "I know of no one to whom I can better entrust the care of this work than You, my Jesus, who have such great zeal for Your Mother's glory. Therefore I dedicate it and recommend it to You."

And we must never forget the consoling truth revealed by the Holy Spirit: *"He that honoreth his mother is as one that layeth up a treasure"* (Ec 3:5). If this applies to one who honors his earthly mother, how much more will it hold true for one who honors our heavenly Mother? Moreover, motherhood and queenship cannot be separated in Our Lady. She is Queen because she is Mother of God, and she could not be Mother of God without being Queen.

It means a great deal to us, also, that this heavenly Queen is a Mother whose sweetness and kindness goes beyond that of any earthly mother. A Queen, who proves to be a Mother full of tenderness for her children, commands more admiration than if she were merely a mother. Queenship adds a glory to motherhood, as motherhood makes the Queen more loving.

In the sacred Liturgy, the Church sings to Mary, "Ave Regina coelorum" — "Hail Queen of Heaven!"

We, too, should sing thus, earnestly desiring in our hearts that as *"every glory and honor"* should be paid to Christ our King (Heb 2:9), so also it might be rendered to our Mother and Queen.

Journeying with her toward Paradise

We need to understand that Mary's Queenship demands our devotion as her children and subjects, and that this is in the interests of our salvation. St. Thomas Aquinas gave the clear teaching that "the Mother of God obtained for herself the majesty of royalty so that she may be Queen of mercy while her Son is King of Justice." And who among us is not in need of mercy?

Only he who stands under the Queen's mantle of protection will be a partaker in her victory over the infernal serpent (*"She will crush thy head"* — Gen 3:15). To downgrade her throne of love, therefore, is ingratitude and folly. St. Maximilian M. Kolbe was able to say, "The Immaculate must be the Queen over all nations, and this as soon as possible, and not only over all taken together as a whole, but over each person individually. Whoever goes contrary to this and refuses to believe in her love, will perish. But he who shall acknowledge her as Queen and strive, as her soldier, for the conquest of the world for her — he will live, he will thrive, and will always wonderfully prosper."

We ought to be certain that this is so. The Queen of Victory is not in the least afraid of hell. St. Veronica Giuliani was often attacked by the devil, even physically; but if she invoked Our Lady, the devil, taking flight, would howl, "Do not invoke my enemy." When, in a vision she had at Lourdes, St. Bernadette was terrified at seeing a band of devils who were giving hellish howls near her, a single severe glance at them from the Immaculate Queen was enough to make them flee.

One day the pastor and Servant of God, Don Edward Poppe, was called to minister to a very sick man in his parish. Someone warned him in advance that he was dealing with an unbeliever full of bitter hate.

"Never mind," the priest said. "We will send him off to Paradise."

As he entered the sick man's room, he saw a little statue of the Immaculate. At once he lit a candle before it and began aloud to beg Our Lady to deliver that soul from the devil's clutches.

He left, without saying anything. But he returned the next day. As soon as he arrived he heard the sick man ask, "Father, do you want a match?" The pastor, shocked and deeply moved, accepted the match, lit the candle, and began to pray.

After a short time, the unbeliever called him to come close to him. Then he said, "Father, I would now like to go to Confession. Our Lady and you are stronger than the devil."

Our Lady is beyond doubt an all-powerful Queen, *"fearsome as an army in battle array"* (Cant 6:3).

St. Maximilian Mary Kolbe wrote that today "the serpent lifts up his head throughout the world, but the Immaculate is crushing his head with her overwhelming victories." We also have the consoling promise given by Our Lady at Fatima: "In the end my Immaculate Heart will triumph."

Yes, O Mary, Mother of God, Sovereign Virgin, God's most glorious boast, we will follow you as our Queen of love, You who are all-powerful and all-heavenly, all-affectionate and all-bright — *Salve Regina!*

OUR LADY IS MEDIATRIX

The first action of Mary recorded in the Gospel is her visit to her cousin St. Elizabeth (Lk 1:39–56). After the Incarnation of the Word within her virginal body, Our Lady then began to accomplish her first act, an act of *mediation*. She went to visit St. Elizabeth bringing Jesus into that home in order to instill sanctifying grace into the soul of John the Baptist while still being carried within his mother's womb.

Our Lady brings Jesus to us and takes us to Jesus. That is why we call her Mediatrix between Jesus and ourselves, between grace and souls. Her role as Mediatrix is like that of the mother of a family who, by her toil and sacrifice, merits and receives all the earnings of the father of the family in order to use them as she thinks best according to the needs of the home.

St. Maximilian M. Kolbe took this truth so much to heart that he ardently hoped for a dogmatic definition. He wrote, taught, prayed, and had others pray, that the time would soon come when the Church would solemnly proclaim as a dogma of our faith, Mary's role as Mediatrix and Co-Redemptrix. And St. Padre Pio of Pietrelcina, in saying his hundred Rosaries a day, offered evidence that all the graces that were drawing souls to him from every part of the world, that were enlightening, converting, saving, and sanctifying them, were graces he was obtaining from the divine Mediatrix by means of the Rosary.

She brings us Jesus

If *"the wages of sin is death"* (Rom 6:23), the wages earned by the Redemption are life, that is, Jesus and His grace, the supernatural life of the soul: *"I am … the life"* (Jn 11:25).

It is Our Lady who brings us Jesus and wins for us His grace, just as it was she who carried Jesus into St. Elizabeth's home and brought sanctifying grace to the soul of the infant John the Baptist, who *"leaped in his mother's womb"* (Lk 1:41).

By her response, *"Be it done to me according to thy word"* (Lk 1:38), to the angel's announcement, Our Lady accepted the role of uniting God and mankind. Her immaculate, virginal womb was the place where God and human race encountered and were reconciled.

Her role, her mission as Mediatrix with Heaven, was willed by God, according to St. Bernard's celebrated teaching, "God willed that we should receive all grace through Mary." St. Bonaventure, St. Anthony, St. Louis Grignion de Montfort and St. Alphonsus all taught the same. Popes, Doctors and saints have upheld this truth, guaranteeing it to be a heritage of our holy Faith.

St. Leonard of Port Maurice used to say that when trying to open hearts to the way to Jesus in his long and vibrant sermons, "the stroke which the frightening sermon on hell and divine judgment does not make, the sermon on my beloved Mother Mary does." The great missionary St. Francis Xavier bore witness that the pagans were not accepting the Gospel except when Our Lady was presented standing near Jesus on the Cross. Also, the first Gentiles to follow Christ, the royal Magi, who came from the East in search of Jesus — where did they find Him? In the arms of His Mother! *"They found the Child with Mary His Mother"* (Mt 2:11).

"Heart" and "Neck" of the Mystical Body

It has been said that Our Lady is the *heart* of the Mystical Body of Christ because she sends the blood of divine grace to all the members of Christ's Body, and because she is a living portrayal of that motherly affection which she received for us when she became spiritual Mother of the great family, the Church.

With more expressive imagery, though less beautiful, St. Pius X teaches us that if Jesus is the *Head* of the Mystical Body, Our Lady is the *neck* joining Head to Body. The three are not on the same level; for the neck is under the head and over the body. Our Lady is subordinate to the Head (Christ), and is superior to the Body (the Church), but she furnishes a vital connection between the two. As the neck is the link joining head and body, so Our Lady is the link in the union — that is, she is *Mediatrix* — between Jesus and souls, between Christ the Head, and the Church His Body. As a consequence, whatever flows from the Head to the Body (which is the Church) *necessarily and only* passes through the neck. St. Bernardine of Siena could aptly write: "She is the neck of our Head. By means of her all the spiritual gifts are imparted to the Mystical Body." And St. Pio of Pietrelcina confided to his spiritual Father that he felt "closely linked to the Son by means of this Mother."

Thus it is easy to understand how devotion to Our Lady is morally necessary for salvation and for growing in holiness. If it is true that without grace, salvation and holiness are impossible, it is obvious that no one is saved nor becomes holy except through Mary, who has been appointed for every soul, as the channel of the grace of his salvation and holiness.

This was confirmed by Pope Paul VI when he wrote that Our Lady even "now from Heaven continues to fulfill her role and dedicates herself to the development of the divine life in every soul among redeemed mankind. This is a very comforting truth."

One can say, then, without doubt that *Our Lady is Jesus' way of coming to us, and she is every man's way to go to Jesus.* St. Bonaventure confirms this teaching. "Just as God descended to us by means of her, it is necessary that we ascend to God by means of her."

St. Bonaventure speaks of the necessity of devotion to Mary, not of the utility or convenience. Therefore, St. Alphonsus said that lack of devotion to Mary is a *bad sign*, when one is judging whether a man is saved. And St. Leonard of Port Maurice preached plainly, "It is impossible that a person be saved who is not devout toward Mary."

Grace upon grace

Abundant and necessary graces come to us through Mary. There are facts to support beautifully this consoling truth — facts bearing out the limitless extent of Mary's activity in bringing Jesus to souls and souls to Jesus, and in obtaining and distributing to men every grace of whatever type — spiritual, temporal, and corporal graces, as well as the grace of conversion, the grace of a holy life, the grace of healing. What did St. Pio of Pietrelcina say to one who wanted to thank him for graces received? He said, "It is Our Lady who has done the favor. Go thank Our Lady. I am not the one to thank."

St. Louis Grignion de Montfort declared that graces are Our Lady's property, and she disposes of them and gives them out to whom she wills, as she wills, and when she wills. Who can keep count of how may times, without our realizing it, she has united souls to Jesus by opening the gates of sanctifying and purifying grace? We will give just a few examples.

From the time of his youth St. Camillus de Lellis had led a loose life. One day when he was on the road returning from San Giovanni Rotondo, by an inner illumination he saw the wretched state of his soul. It was like being struck with lightning. Such fear seized him that he fell on his knees and began to weep and sob loudly for a long time. "What a wretch I am! How miserable I am! Why did I not know the Lord before? Why have I been so deaf to His calls?" For a full hour he was beside himself, plunged in purifying tears of grief. He understood the priceless value of that ardent repentance. He tried to reflect back to see how he happened to receive such an immense grace on that day, and he remembered that it was February 2nd, the day honoring the Blessed Virgin's Purification. Then he exclaimed, "Oh! Today is February 2nd, the Feast of Our Lady's Purification. Now I know who won this great grace for me."

As a young man St. Francis de Sales suffered an interior turmoil which was destroying him morally and physically. One day in a chapel of Our Lady he appealed desperately to the Mother of Mercy and recited the *Memorare* of St. Bernard. The result of that prayer was immediate. The Saint was delivered at once from his trouble and experienced an indescribable peace, which he never lost.

St. Gabriel of Our Lady of Sorrows, an attractive, chivalrous youth of Spoleto, Italy, who always lived an upright life, was resisting the invitations of grace to aim higher. One day, during a procession in which a statue of the Blessed Virgin was carried, his eyes met those of Our Lady, and he distinctly heard these words, "Francis, Francis! The world is not for you. The religious life is waiting for you." Without delay he finally made up his mind and within a few years he had rapidly advanced in holiness.

Every benefit comes to us by her means

If this is how things are, instead of marveling about Catholics who often turn to Mary, we ought to wonder and grieve over those who do not.

God's mind on this is very clear: Every grace, as well as Christ Himself, comes to us through Mary — every grace, however small or great. The management of the whole supernatural treasury belongs to the Heart of Our Lady. *"The Holy Spirit shall come upon thee"* (Lk 1:35). There is no bestowal of grace that does not depend on her. God has willed it so. In this way, just as the woman, Eve, admitted sin into the human race (cf. Ec 25:33), so another woman, Mary, is the bearer of grace to all mankind.

Therefore we understand the wisdom of the saints in appealing to Mary in their every undertaking and in entrusting to Mary every duty, every enterprise, everything! We have recourse to the *Mother of Divine Grace* to assure the presence of grace for us in everything.

When St. Pio of Pietrelcina used to come down for Confessions every day, before he reached the confessional he would pass by a picture of the Immaculate. Without fail he would stop for a few minutes to pray before it. He was entrusting to Our Lady the Confessions that he was about to hear and was appealing for an abundance of graces. The fruitful results of his priestly ministry were the concrete answers to his prayer.

Thus one should well appreciate how precious is the devout habit of saying the Hail Mary before our ordinary and our extraordinary undertakings. A Hail Mary before study, before work, before giving a talk, before an examination, before a journey, before surgery, before meals, before rest, etc., is an assurance of a grace that elevates and sanctifies the action.

This holy practice is unpopular today, as it has been in other times. But the theological reasons that support it cannot be met by excuses from people who would want some other prayer substituted for the Hail Mary. If the grace for something well done comes to me from Mary, is it not right to call on Mary directly? Now it is precisely the Hail Mary (or another Marian invocation) that serves this purpose.

Bl. Contardo Ferrini, for example, had this magnificent rule of life: "Before every conversation I will recommend myself to Heaven with a Hail Mary; likewise before meals." St. Gabriel of Our Lady of Sorrows, when he entered or was to leave his cell, would say a Hail Mary on his knees, asking Our Lady's blessing and entrusting to her what he was about to do. How many saints have there not been who did this before every activity!

Above all, in moments of danger one should never fail to turn to Our Lady. St. Peter Julian Eymard made it his rule to say a Hail Mary whenever he faced a temptation. The heavenly Mother's aid is a decisive factor, if we appeal to her. St. Alphonsus said that if someone prudently doubted that he had consented to sin, but had appealed to Our Lady during the temptation, he could be sure he did not fall from grace.

Let us put ourselves in the care of the Mother of Grace at every hour and every moment and forbid that she would lament of having her hands full of graces to give us, only to find that we neither want them nor do we ask for them — as reproached by St. Catherine Labouré.

Without speaking of other Marian shrines, it is enough just to remember Lourdes in order to be convinced that Our Lady is really the true Mother of all graces, that she is the heavenly Treasurer, the royal Dispenser of every spiritual and temporal favor. Hence we ought to turn to her with faith and confidence. She has a heart full of sympathy for us. The Church even tells us so in applying to Mary's mediation this inspired verse: *"Let us go with confidence to the throne of grace: that we may obtain mercy and find grace in seasonable aid"* (Heb 4:16).

Hence St. Margaret Mary Alacoque never wanted to ask anything of Jesus except by means of His Mother, our Mediatrix. And St. Cajetan asserted, "We can ask any favor of the Lord, but we cannot obtain it without Mary's intercession."

The Fashioner of the Saints

The most beautiful, the most precious favors that Our Lady loves to grant her children are certainly the graces to become holy.

St. Albert the Great wrote: "The Blessed Virgin draws the sinner, enlightens the repentant, and guides the innocent." But her deepest, fondest interest is in forming saints, in transforming men into her Son Jesus, who is the whole reason for her existence. She alone can make us become like her Son. St. Bernadine of Siena wrote, "The perfect soul becomes so only by means of Mary." It cannot be otherwise.

As a mother stays near her child from the time of his birth until he is mature and is settled down, so Our Lady is the Fashioner of every saint. She rears him from birth until he *"stand in all things perfect"* (cf. Eph 6:13). It is always the mother who takes care of her children at every stage of their growth, provided they are docile to her motherly efforts. The development of holiness is the work of grace. Our Lady is the Mother of Divine Grace, the Mediatrix of every grace, the Spouse of the sanctifying Spirit. Therefore sanctification, or the development of holiness, is the work of her immaculate hands that bear Jesus; it is the work of her Heart filled with the Holy Spirit. Our Lady is the heavenly plant from which the *White Rose* blossomed forth, which is Jesus, with all the saints of Heaven.

St. Maximilian M. Kolbe declares, *"It can be said that all the Saints are the work of the Blessed Virgin, and that a special devotion to her is their common characteristic."*

St. Teresa of Jesus, that queen of mysticism, wonderfully described from personal experience the soul's journey toward perfection all the way to the summits of holiness. She assures us that Our Lady's presence continues during all the stages of the spiritual life. This seraphic Saint of Carmel declares that her own development in the way of holiness began when she gave herself to Mary; that it continued with Mary's assistance during the stages of purification without interruption; and that Mary closely guided her soul from its entrance into the *Interior Castle* all the way to its center, where God is. Our Lady's assistance is necessary in order to win the battles one must go through, especially to gain the humility needed in order to get beyond the narrow gate of worthy prayer. It is Our Lady who, with her graces, accompanies the soul into the prayer of quiet, who moves it on into the ecstatic union, who makes it reach the transforming union, achieving a perfect likeness to Jesus.

We know, too, that the loftiest expressions of the mystical life, such as stigmatization, spiritual marriage, the consummation of love in the bosom of the Trinity — such as occurred to St. Catherine of Siena, St. Veronica Giuliani, St. Gemma Galgani — come about with Mary's mediation and motherly assistance. Why is this so? Because all the perfection that souls gain is contained in Mary, the *sacred treasury of all holiness* (St. Andrew of Crete), the "dwelling place of all Three Divine Persons, and the repository of holiness" (St. Bonaventure).

She delivers from Purgatory

Our Lady is the Mediatrix for the souls suffering in Purgatory as well. She herself revealed to St. Bridgit that her Mediation extends even to Purgatory, and that the favor of a soul's deliverance from those pains comes about through her motherly Heart and her interceding hand.

This teaching is upheld by great saints and Doctors of the Church, such as St. Peter Damian, St. Bonaventure, St. Bernadine of Siena, St. Francis de Sales, St. Alphonsus Liguori.

For example, St. Bernadine calls Mary the "Plenipotentiary" for Purgatory, that is, one who possesses full powers to deliver whoever she wishes. Therefore a prayer to Our Lady in behalf of those souls is a hopeful encouragement to them and truly hastens their deliverance.

St. Teresa of Jesus had a vision of Purgatory when she was reciting her Rosary. She saw that at each Hail

Mary those souls received a spray of cool water that relieved them in their burning torments. The holy Rosary is particularly effective as an appeal for them. Our Lady made this consoling promise to Bl. Alan: "For those devoted to the Rosary I will ask for graces and blessings during their time on earth, and after their death I will obtain a great comfort for them. Every day I deliver a great number of these souls from Purgatory and bring them home to Heaven." St. Alphonsus gave this wise and earnest recommendation: "If we want to help the souls in Purgatory, let us say the Rosary for them, which brings them great comfort." And in the life of St. Pompilius Pirrotti we read that the Saint recited the Rosary with the souls in Purgatory, who gave the responses aloud and showed that they experienced great comfort from it.

Let us, too, make use of this prayer to relieve those suffering souls and to win for them the deliverance that they long for. Once when St. Pio of Pietrelcina was giving a Rosary to someone he said, "I am giving you a treasure. Know how to appreciate and treasure it. Let us empty Purgatory." How precious this *treasure* is and how little it costs to have it!

It is especially on the Marian feasts and on Saturdays that Our Lady is generous in delivering souls from Purgatory.

St. Peter Damian, St. Ildefonse, and St. Frances of Rome assure us that it is on the Feast of the Assumption of the Blessed Virgin Mary above all, that a great number of souls leave Purgatory in a joyous procession that adds a new glory for the heavenly Queen.

It is right to expect that, among the souls in Purgatory, Our Lady will show a preference for those who have been devoted to her. The holy Virgin said to Bl. Alan, "I am a Mother to the souls in Purgatory, and each hour through my prayers the pains of those devoted to me are lightened." Can we imagine what a comfort it must be for souls devoted to her when this kind Mother visits that place of suffering? Wherever she comes, she brings an abundance of graces, and those suffering souls are waiting for her motherly mediation which delivers them from their torments and brings them to Heaven.

OUR LADY IS THE GATE OF HEAVEN

We ought to have devotion to Our Lady because it is a guarantee of eternal salvation and a sign of predestination to Paradise.

St. Augustine said that all the predestined on earth are enclosed in the womb of Mary.

St. Bonaventure declared, "Whoever is enrolled among Mary's devotees will be enrolled in the Book of Life." Or, in clearer language, whoever loves Our Lady, has an assurance of Paradise. St. Alphonsus ventured to say, "He who loves Our Lady can be as sure of Paradise as if he were already there."

Devotion to Our Lady, therefore, is the assurance of the Kingdom of Heaven. Our Lady is called the "Gate of Heaven" because one does not enter Paradise except through her. Thus St. Bonaventure said in his concise way, "No one can enter Paradise unless he passes through Mary, who is the gate." It is a consoling thought that everybody can be devoted to Our Lady and thus keep close to this "Gate of Heaven" — both the saint and the sinner, the believer and the unbeliever.

Our Lady is the Mother of all. She is the Mediatrix for whoever wants to be saved. She is the Queen of Love over all the world. If God the Father *wants all men to be saved"* (I Ti 2:4), Our Lady, the Mother of all, likewise desires that everybody gain eternal salvation. And if Jesus says that He gives His sheep *"life everlasting, and they shall not perish forever; and no man shall pluck them out of My hand"* (Jn 10:28), then Mary, the heavenly Coredemptrix, will never allow the devil to snatch any of her devoted clients from her hands. *"He that shall find me shall find life, and shall have salvation from the Lord"* (Pr 8:35): thus the Church refers to the Blessed Virgin Mary in the Liturgy.

Refuge of sinners

It is a consoling thing to know that God has entrusted to the heavenly Mother above all else the salvation of people in sin, of souls led astray, of souls in despair, who turn to her for help.

St. Gertrude saw the holy Virgin in a vision wearing a great mantle, and many animals of every kind appeared under it, seeking refuge. Our Lady gave her to understand that all sinners who appeal to her were finding refuge and salvation.

Great saints and Doctors of the Church assure us of this truth with words that offer great hope to troubled hearts. We present some of their thoughts.

St. Ignatius the Martyr says, "One who is always full of zeal and devotion for the Virgin Mother of God will never come to a bad end. It is impossible, O

Virgin, for a sinner to be saved except through your help and protection."

St. Augustine declares that "Mary is the only hope of sinners." And St. Hilary, speaking of true devotion to Our Lady, counsels us by saying that "no matter how sinful one may have been, if he has devotion to Mary it is impossible that he be lost."

St. Peter Damian states, "O Mary, it is possible for you to bring back the hope of salvation even to the most despairing souls." And St. Anselm adds, "O Mary, it is impossible that anyone who has recourse to you should perish."

St. Bernard uses the beautiful Biblical images of the ark and the ladder: "Mary," he writes, "is the ark by means of which one escapes the shipwreck of eternal damnation. My dear sons, Mary ... is the ladder of sinners; she is my great assurance; she is the whole reason for my hope."

We should also remember that St. Bonaventure, St. Louis Grignion, St. Paul of the Cross, St. Alphonsus Liguori, St. Leonard of Port Maurice, the holy Curé of Ars, St. Anthony Claret, and many others confirm this doctrine.

But the whole teaching on this truth seems to be summed up in this clear statement of St. John Damascene: "God bestows the grace of devotion to Our Lady on those whom He wills to save."

For this reason, St. Alphonsus was unwearying in urging those having a devotion to Our Lady to gratefully preserve this sweet pledge of eternal salvation. When people came to see him or when he met people, he gave them a little image of Our Lady and exhorted them to have devotion to the Mother of all mercies. We who are sinners should never forget St. Camillus de Lellis' remark: "Woe to us sinners if we were not to have this great Advocate in Heaven!"

She saves souls from hell

Another consoling assurance that the Saints gave us is Mary's boundless, merciful charity toward those devoted to her who, according to justice, would deserve hell.

There is a chorus of strong voices from St. John Chrysostom to St. Bernard, from St. Alphonsus to St. Maximilian M. Kolbe, who teach that, while Jesus is King of Mercy and Justice, Our Lady is Queen of Mercy only.

St. John Chrysostom forcefully and clearly declared, "Mary's immense mercy saves a great number of unhappy persons who, according to the norms of divine justice, would be damned."

The mother of St. Thérèse of Lisieux reports a charming episode from the life of her holy daughter: "Little Teresa asked me one day if she would go to Paradise. I answered, 'Yes, if you are nice and good.' Then she said, 'Ah, Mother, then if I am not good, will I go to hell? But I know what I would do then.

When you go away to Heaven I will go with you; and you would hold me real tight in your arms. Then that would make the good God take me…' I read in her expression that she was convinced that the good God could do nothing against her if she stayed in her mother's arms."

Perhaps everyone knows the instructive story which St. Pio of Pietrelcina used to recount so often: "Our Lord walks through Paradise, and He encounters the faces of many sinners worthy of hell and not of Paradise. He calls St. Peter and warns him to be more attentive not to let anyone into Paradise who is not worthy. St. Peter promises to be more vigilant and attentive.

"The next day, Our Lord takes another walk, and again He encounters many sinners. He calls St. Peter again, and this time severely admonishes him. St. Peter feels humiliated, and promises Him the maximum vigilance."

"But the next day, the same thing happens: Our Lord encounters new sinners in Paradise. This time He calls St. Peter, determined to punish him and snatch the keys of Paradise away from him. But St. Peter knows how to defend himself, because he discovered the way in which sinners are entering Paradise; and he relates to Our Lord that, in the dark of the night, while all are sleeping, Our Blessed Lady opens the doors of Heaven and lets in those sinners. 'Well,' St. Peter concludes, 'with Your Mother, I cannot do anything'"; and Our Lord adds: 'And neither can I!'"[5]

St. Gregory the Great rightly declared, "Nothing resists your power, O Mary, and your Son appears to be fulfilling a duty when He grants your prayers." It cannot be that Jesus stands against His Mother.

In the life of St. Gemma we read that one day during an ecstasy the Saint asked Jesus for the conversion of an obstinate sinner who was a high ranking mason. Jesus would not hear of it. "He has abused grace too much. He is hardened in his evil way. I have abandoned him."

St. Gemma did not give up. She appealed again, but had no success. Finally, in view of Jesus' decisive refusal, the Saint exclaimed disappointedly, "Very well. I understand, Jesus. I will speak to Your Mother. And it is up to You to say no to her!" She spoke to His Mother. Our Lady cast a glance at Jesus, and Jesus

---

5 *Translator's note*: This parable is intended to carry a message of hope for the unpresumptuous, and not to favor presumption. Speakers have therefore wisely qualified it by the following account presented as true history by St. Alphonsus Liguori: In the year 1611 on the Vigil of Pentecost, a great throng of people had gathered at the celebrated shrine of Our Lady at Montevergine. They profaned the feast with scandalous dances, insobriety, and immodesty. Suddenly it was noticed that a fire had broken out in the wooden frame clubhouse where they had gathered. In less than a half-hour it was reduced to ashes and more than 1500 people perished. Five persons who escaped testified under oath that they had seen our Blessed Lady herself setting the fire with two torches. — *Glories of Mary*, Part 2, Ossequio 5 (cf. Gal 6:7).

smiled: the grace was effected. On that very day the sinner went to Confession.

St. Bernard wisely exclaimed, "Mary is the whole reason for our hope!" Let us never grow tired, therefore, of confidently calling on Our Lady, saying with St. Ephrem, "Hail, O hope for the soul! O secure stronghold of Christians! Hail, O help of sinners! Hail, O Bulwark of the faithful, Refuge of all the world!"

All-Powerful in prayer

The best proof of the consoling truth that Mary's prayer is all-powerful, is found in the Gospel account of the marriage feast of Cana. Our Lady's intervention when God's time had not arrived (*"My hour has not yet come"* — Jn 2:4), and the fact that she yet easily obtained the unobtainable, assures us that her mercy is truly all-powerful with the Heart of God, to the point of making Him change the divine decrees. Thus St. Thomas Aquinas wrote, "By those words that Jesus spoke at Cana, 'My hour has not yet come,' Jesus meant that He assuredly would not have performed the miracle if someone other than the Virgin had requested it; but because the request came from His Mother, He granted it at once."

If Our Lady was so considerate of others and appealed for them so successfully at the marriage feast of Cana, how much more considerate will she not be, and how much more all-powerful will her prayer not be, on occasions that are far more serious for souls and for humanity? Would it be possible for us to doubt that this is so? Such a doubt would be unreasonable. Our Lady is always a devoted Mother who is watchful and knowledgeable and guards against dangers, and leaves no stone unturned to protect her children from them. Who knows how many times she has succeeded in changing the divine decrees in order to save us from some punishment we deserved!

On the night of March 21, 1812, Bl. Anna Maria Taigi was pouring out her prayers because of the ill fortunes of the Church and humanity. She then had a vision. She saw the earth as a globe in the midst of flames that were about to destroy it. She also saw Jesus on His Cross, shedding His Blood, while the Blessed Virgin Mary was at the foot of it. Mary was praying that by the merits of that Blood which she was offering for sinners, the terrible punishments might come to a halt. And mercy was obtained. St. Colette, a Poor Clare nun, had a similar vision.

Some centuries before that, when St. Gregory the Great was Pope, a terrible epidemic broke out in Rome. Every day thousands of people died. St. Gregory ordered that there be a penitential procession from the Basilica of St. Mary Major to St. Peter's. The Pope processed barefoot, wearing a penitential garb and carrying an image of Our Lady in his hands. When the procession had passed through the city and reached the *Bridge of the Holy Angel*, the voices of a choir of

Angels were heard singing in the heavens what is now the Church's Marian Antiphon in the Easter liturgy:

> *Queen of Heaven rejoice, alleluia!*
> *Christ, whom you bore, alleluia,*
> *Has risen as He said, alleluia!*

St. Gregory at once added the invocation, "Pray to God for us, alleluia!"

Then a warrior angel became visible as he put his sword back into its scabbard. At that moment, the plague ceased to take victims. Hence that bridge was given the name *Ponte Sant'Angelo.*

Only in Paradise will we appreciate the immensity of Mary's merciful and boundless power. And then we will sing to her an eternal hymn of thanksgiving. We could not do otherwise.

In the meantime, while we remain in this poor world of thorns and thistles we ought to have trust in the all-powerful intercession of our devoted Mother for our personal needs, for those of our family and of society, and for any and every need, provided we are turning to her and trusting in her with the devotedness of children.

Who can ever count, for example, the number of times Our Lady delivered St. John Bosco out of the troubles he faced? Once it happened that the baker refused to bring him any more bread for his hungry boys unless the Saint paid what he owed, which was a considerable sum. St. John Bosco had no money, and begged the baker to bring the bread anyway, because Our Lady would see that the debt was paid during the course of the day. The baker came expected to be paid, but the Saint was hearing Confessions, whereupon the baker left, intending return later. After the Confessions the Saint begged Our Lady to help him, for he did not know what to do. At that moment, an unknown gentleman appeared who gave the Saint a sealed letter. Don Bosco put the letter in his breviary without opening it, and went to celebrate Holy Mass. After Mass, he went to the refectory reflecting on his debt to the baker when, suddenly, he remembered the letter in his breviary. Upon opening it, the Saint found a generous offering sufficient to satisfy the baker.

"In me is all hope of life and of virtue."

(Ec 24:25)

Chapter III

HOW IS DEVOTION TO OUR LADY LIVED?

- ◆ **Honoring Our Lady**

- ◆ **Loving Our Lady**

- ◆ **Imitating Our Lady**

HONORING OUR LADY

Veneration paid to Our Lady must not be a veneration of simply any kind you please. Rather, it should be an immense and strong filial veneration.

Our Lady is Jesus' Mother and our Mother, lofty in her dignity, sublime in her holiness, and rich in "heavenly gifts above all the angelic spirits and far above all the Saints" (Bl. Pius IX, *Ineffabilis Deus*).

Our Lady is the woman preëminently *"full of grace,"* as she was hailed by St. Gabriel the Archangel (Lk 1:28). St. Andrew of Crete wrote, "O Virgin, you are without an equal, O Saint holier than any saint, O sacred treasury of all holiness!" And St. Peter Damian: "Any creature, however great, is inferior to Mary. The Creator alone surpasses this creature."

How can anyone not see the duty of honoring such a sublime creature, given us from God's hand in order to enthrall Heaven and earth?

The need to honor her

God himself taught us veneration for Our Lady when he sent an Angel to ask her consent for the Incarnation. The angel Gabriel, too, instructs us when he greets her with words that tell of her grace and speak her praise. The matron, St. Elizabeth teaches us when, on meeting Our Lady, she exclaims, *"How have I deserved to be thus visited by the Mother of my Lord? ... blessed art thou ..."* (Lk 1:43, 45). St. Joseph, too, teaches us a lesson, as he stands by her in a silence which is filled with devoted veneration. We learn a lesson from the faith and piety of the Christian people who, down the centuries, have erected shrines, churches, and chapels honoring her, she who prophesied under divine inspiration, *"All generations shall call me blessed"* (Lk 1:48). We learn this from all the Saints who inhabited this earth, seeing how they celebrated Mary's boundless love. Who could ever enumerate all the acts of veneration offered to the heavenly Mother throughout these two thousand years of faith and love? All this tells us that devotion to Our Lady, besides being a duty, has been a *necessity*, and is surely a *necessity* for every Christian. We know that the Church has always felt this universal *need* and has expressed it with a beautiful array of Marian feasts and celebrations placed on the calendar, in harmony with the mysteries of Christ.

Thus the whole Church is inspired and directed more and more to pay Our Lady the high honor of reverence and praise which we call the liturgical cult. Pope Paul VI's Apostolic exhortation entitled *The Cult of the Blessed Virgin* happily confirms Mary's honored place in the liturgy and the Christian's duty to honor the heavenly Queen in the liturgy, as well as in devout practices of Marian piety.

What the saints have done

We will now give some examples of veneration which the saints have paid to the Mother of God.

With ardent zeal St. Bernard paid reverence to Our Lady and with his gifted pen he sung her praises so well that he earned the title *Mary's minstrel*. His fervor and devotion were such as to keep him occupied all day on Marian feasts, in the interests of Our Lady, so that he forgot everything else, even very important business, such as replying to urgent letters from the Pope.

St. Francis of Assisi offered so many beautiful acts of veneration to Our Lady as beyond counting. Every day, he recited the Office of the Blessed Virgin and prepared for her feasts with special prayers and penances. He reverenced her altars and her images and composed praises and prayers to Mary that overflowed with his seraphic warmth and tenderness.

St. Louis Grignion de Montfort was a completely Marian Saint. When he wrote *True Devotion to Mary*, he became the great teacher of devotion to Our Lady. His whole life was a wonderful example of devotion to the heavenly Queen. As a young boy, he would spend hours, every day that he could, before an image of Our Lady of Peace. Later, as an adult he never wearied of praying the Rosary, and he preached devotion to Mary all over France.

What shall we say of St. Alphonsus Liguori, author of *The Glories of Mary,* a veritable *monument* of veneration which he constructed for the Queen of Heaven and which will remain forever in the Church? The Saint's profound and sweet veneration is also contagiously evident in his devout Marian hymns and in his little work called *Visits to Blessed Mary*, printed in the same volume as his *Visits to the Blessed Sacrament,* and enhanced with a Marian fragrance. God only could count the acts of veneration this Saint paid to the Mother of God every day of his long life.

The holy Curé of Ars, St. John Vianney, who owed his priestly ordination to his tender devotion to Our Lady and his assiduous use of the holy Rosary, filled his life with love and veneration for Our Lady. When he became a pastor, one of first things he did was to consecrate his parish to Our Lady and dedicate the first chapel he built to her. In his frugal bedroom, together with a Crucifix, he kept an image of the Immaculate before which he was often raised to ecstatic prayer.

These are only a few examples of veneration paid to Our Lady on the part of some saints. We could find as many more examples as there are saints; for it is impossible for a saint not to feel the need of venerating Our Lady. It is a filial need that is lovable and sweet!

Venerate her in every way possible

Deeds and acts that venerate Our Lady range from the grandest and most solemn to the simplest and most ordinary.

To establish two little *cities* of the Immaculate entirely consecrated to her, as St. Maximilian M. Kolbe did in Poland and Japan, is certainly not something for all to do. To build splendid churches in the Blessed Virgin's honor as, for example, St. John Bosco did in Turin, and Bl. Bartolo Longo did in Pompei, are impressive deeds of veneration which few can accomplish.

Likewise to dedicate to the Blessed Mother a convent of consecrated virgins and cultivate it as a *dovecote of the Virgin,* holding up Our Lady as the prioress of the community, as St. Teresa of Jesus did — this is no ordinary veneration, but it is extraordinary and not possible for just anybody.

We must say the same of the founding of religious Orders, Congregations and Associations to honor Mary; also of the composition or execution of various Marian works — books, paintings, works of sculpture and of music, and of the dedication of chapels and altars to the Blessed Virgin. Three have been Saints and clients of Mary who have done all this, especially dedicating chapels and altars — as, for example, St. Bonaventure, St. Cajetan and St. Alphonsus, down to the recent Bl. Don Orione, the Servant of God Don Alberione, and St. Pio of Pietrelcina. Also, that seraphic lover of the Holy Eucharist, St. Juliana Falconieri, not only did this, but left as a duty for her Sisters that "in every church of our Order there be a chapel or altar in honor of Our Lady."

While not everybody can offer Our Lady these great accomplishments of veneration, all can do ordinary deeds of veneration that extend to little things like praying daily to Our Lady, honoring images of Mary, visiting Marian shrines, chapels, and altars, paying reverence, as by a tip of the hat, to arranging flowers to adorn images of Mary; devoutly cherishing a little altar or picture of Our Lady in our home; keeping a Rosary in our pocket, a Marian medal around our neck, a little picture of Our Lady in our wallet or purse, or in a book we are reading, or on our work-table…

Who is unable to do such things?

Small examples

Above all, we should have the interest to venerate Our Lady by the frequent, devout recitation of the *Hail Mary*. St. Thomas Aquinas had such an earnest esteem for the *Hail Mary* that, one year, he preached on it throughout the whole of Lent. St. Lawrence of Brindisi did the same.

One cannot find a lovelier prayer for honoring the heavenly Mother. St. Lucy Filippini said that the *Hail Mary* pleases Our Lady because by it she was greeted as the Mother of God by the Angel Gabriel and by St. Elizabeth. Whereas we ourselves recall those two fascinating young female Saints — St. Catherine of Siena and St. Thérèse of the Child Jesus, together with those two marvelous young boys — St. Aloysius Gonzaga and St. Gerard Majella — who would recite the *Hail Mary* while going up the stairs, and perhaps even kneeling down at every step. St. Alphonsus Liguori, St. Leonard of Port Maurice, St. Vincent Pallotti, St. Gabriel of the Sorrowful Mother, the Holy Curé of Ars, and many other saints, would recite the *Hail Mary* every time the clock would strike the hour. And how many saints would recite the *Hail Mary* before every action, before meals, and before rest or recreation?

The *Hail Mary* could blossom on our lips with great ease, could keep us company everywhere like a constant gaze of the soul on Mary and of Mary on the soul. St. Bernadine assures us: "Know that when you greet the Blessed Virgin with the words 'Hail Mary,' immediately she greets you in return."

Regarding the domestic worship towards Our Lady, let us remember the example of the family of St. Maximilian M. Kolbe. Notwithstanding the lack of space in their home, there was always a small corner with a small altar upon which an image of Mary Most Holy was kept, where the whole family would daily unite for prayers in common. In that blessed corner, little Maximilian would spend a long time in prayer, and his love for Our Lady would place deep roots in his heart, in order to bring forth its marvelous fruits one day.

If all Christian homes would return to this holy tradition of setting aside a little altar to Mary for the family prayers, the families would blossom again under the loving gaze and smile of Mary!

Regarding the veneration of the little shrines of the Blessed Virgin, let us remember the example of St. Bernadine of Siena who, as a youth, would set out every evening for his appointment with the Queen of hearts, before an image of Mary Most Holy, located outside the walls of the city. His good aunt — who had no idea at all who this person was with whom the youth would meet outside the city — was very much moved when she, secretly following him, she saw him prostrated in loving veneration before the image of the Holy Virgin.

Likewise, it must have been as equally edifying to witness another young boy along the streets of Pietrelcina, going to and from school, silent and recollected, never failing to pause along the road to pray before a little shrine of the Heavenly Mother. That boy would one day be St. Pio of Pietrelcina, great lover of the *Beautiful Virgin*. And also at Foggia, as a young priest, Padre Pio would set out every day to make a visit to *Our Lady of the seven veils*, the miraculous image that once caused St. Alphonsus Liguori to go into ecstasy while preaching.

Similarly, St. Leopold of Castelnuovo took a brief walk every day at Padua for the purpose of visiting an image of Mary in the parish church of the Holy Cross. St. Pius X, too, sanctified his afternoon walks with a devout visit to the Immaculate in a Lourdes' grotto, replicated in the Vatican gardens. Let us not let these examples be for naught!

Flowers for Mary

To offer flowers to Mary has always been one of the most benign acts of adoration to which the saints have given much importance.

Even as a youngster, St. Crispin would work in a shop every Saturday and received a silver coin as a gift; he would immediately run to buy a beautiful bunch of fresh flowers everytime. The florist became curious to know his reason for buying flowers each Saturday. So one time, he secretly followed the saintly boy and discovered that he immediately took the flowers to the Blessed Virgin's chapel in the church and there, with face all transfigured, he decorated the altar with love.

St. Gabriel of the Sorrowful Mother also took this practice very much to heart. There was not a day, no matter how difficult the conditions were, that he would not find a flower for Mary. He himself would cultivate them in a little flower garden and, many times, while taking care of the plants, he would be heard whispering, almost overcome with love: "My Mary… my Mary…"

Together with St. Crispin and with St. Gabriel of the Sorrowful Mother, we should also call to mind

St. Thérèse who, already at five years of age, loved to decorate with flowers the little altar of Our Lady in her house; we should also remember St. Paschal Baylon, St. Bernadette, St. Dominic Savio, St. Maria Goretti and many other saints. Even St. Leopold of Castelnuovo was anxious to put fresh flowers every day before the little Madonna that he kept in his small confession cell.

Here is another delightful example. Little Joan of Arc, the angelic peasant girl, would gather a bunch of fresh flowers every day to place before a image of Our Lady. Even during the winter season, she would search all over the thickets of the field in order to find some flowers. But it used to happen that she would not find anything because the cold would make all the flowers die. What did she do then? She did not give up hope but, with sublime simplicity, removed some balls of wool from her sheep and offered them to her precious Madonna. How one loves!

At least a sign of veneration

Let us insist on the need to venerate Our Lady, at least with at least some sign of veneration. Justly we demand this because the mercy of Mary is such that even a tiny act of veneration would be sufficient to save one's soul from hell. Let us call to mind some examples.

A lady in the throes of desperation approached the Holy Curé of Ars one day because her husband, an unbeliever, committed suicide by throwing himself out of a window. Immediately upon seeing the woman, the Holy Curé of Ars approached her and, without being asked, said to her: "Madam, your husband is saved, he is saved... Before the mortal blow, Our Lady gave him time to make an act of contrition... Remember that, during the month of May, he would decorate an image of Mary with flowers and consented to pray to her even though being far from believing?... For this veneration towards the Holy Virgin, he obtained salvation and is now in Purgatory in need of suffrages."

A small act of veneration to Our Lady can obtain eternal salvation. Do we think about it?

It once happened to St. Joseph Cafasso, the Saint of those condemned to the gallows, that a condemned criminal obstinately refused the Sacraments, and there was practically nothing that could be done about it. The guards came to bring the criminal to the gallows. Along the way there was a little shrine of Our Lady. Passing before it, the condemned man glanced at the image and made a beautiful bow to the Virgin in accord with a pious habit to which he was accustomed. Immediately when St. Joseph Cafasso saw the condemned criminal make that act of veneration to Our Lady, he exclaimed, convinced and moved: *"He is saved, he is saved. Our Lady will save him!"* He approached him and immediately succeeded in hearing his Confession before his execution.

The same thing happened to a youth from Naples who had the same pious habit of greeting every image of the Blessed Virgin with the words *Hail Mary*. Although being a slave to his vices, Our Lady obtained for him the grace to meet with St. Francis De Gironimo who reconciled him to God before his death.

St. John Berchmans was right when he said: "To merit the protection of Mary, the smallest act of veneration would be enough, provided that it is performed with consistency."

Let us also choose

Let us also choose some particular acts of veneration to Our Lady. Let us choose that which we are capable of doing and then make efforts to be faithful in fulfilling it. Generosity and faithfulness should go together. It would not be good, however, to propose to do much and then to end up being faithful in little or nothing. Let us propose instead to do as much as we are capable of doing with generosity.

If it pleases us, we would do well to choose from among the acts of Marian veneration which the saints have done, and we have many choices! Besides those already mentioned, we wish to present more of them here, and gradually include even more in the following pages.

The Bl. Anna Maria Taigi, mother of seven children, established the practice in her family that the initial morning greeting to one another would be: "Praised be Jesus and Mary."

St. Vincent Pallotti would greet Our Lady every time he would enter or leave his room. St. Alphonsus de Liguori could not leave or enter the house without pausing to greet Our Lady.

St. Margaret Mary Alacoque would make seven genuflections every day and recite seven Hail Marys for the Sorrows of Our Lady. St. Gabriel of the Sorrowful Mother would recite them with his arms stretched out in the form of a cross.

St. John Baptist De Rossi would always carry an image of Mary on his breast. And the Holy Curé of Ars, already as a boy, would sleep with a small statue of Our Lady held tightly against his chest.

Bl. Contardo Ferrini was very faithful in making a daily visit to an altar of Mary Most Holy.

St. Catherine Labouré would present herself many times a day in the chapel to greet Jesus and Our Lady.

The Servant of God, Don Poppe, would inscribe *Hail Mary!* as the heading on every letter he wrote. St. Thomas Aquinas would begin using a pen by writing the name *Mary!* St. Peter M. Chanel would write the name of Mary on his books and notebooks, and even succeeded in convincing his schoolmates to do likewise.

St. Joseph Moscati, the great Neapolitan doctor, would always carry the Holy Rosary in his waistcoat; before he would give an answer or perform an action of consequence, he would finger the Rosary or kiss it. He was also very faithful about making a daily visit to an image of Our Lady of Good Counsel.

Merely on hearing the name of Mary, St. Paul of the Cross used to take off his hat out of reverence.

St. Maximilian M. Kolbe used to place his watch and eye-glasses at the foot of a little statue of the Immaculate each evening. By this gesture he meant to entrust to her all the time and space at his disposal.

St. Bernadette made this recommendation: "Every night when you go to sleep, take your Rosary and doze off reciting it. Do as infants do who doze off calling out 'Mommy! Mommy!'"

Each evening St. Gemma Galgani would not go to sleep without first asking Our Lady's blessing. Likewise Bl. Angela of Foligno and St. Stanislaus Kostka used to give Our Lady an affectionate kiss in the morning and in the evening, and ask her blessing. Once when Bl. Angela asked this blessing, she heard Our Lady reply, "May you be blessed by me and by my Son."

Many other forms of veneration to Mary practiced by the saints could be mentioned. But what is important is that we pledge ourselves to never let a day of our life pass without doing some act of veneration to honor our heavenly Mother and Queen.

LOVING OUR LADY

A few days before his death some spiritual sons of St. Pio of Pietrelcina asked him, "Father, say something to us."

The friar answered, "Love Our Lady and bring others to love her. Always say the Rosary."

This was a kind of spiritual last will and testament of Padre Pio — a Marian testament worthy of one who had lived a life of ardent love for the *Beautiful Virgin.*

Padre Pio's response calls to mind an episode in the life of St. Peter M. Chanel. Once the Saint cut his hand; and then, by a sudden inspiration, he took up a pin, dipped the point into his own blood, and wrote, "Love Mary and make her loved."

Who can ever describe the love of the saints for Our Lady? How could anyone measure it?

The heart of devotion

Let us say first of all that love is, beyond doubt, the heart of devotion to Our Lady. If it is a fact that there can be no true devotion without veneration, then even more so must we say that there can be no true devotion without love. The contrary is inconceivable. The very word *devotion* means *donating oneself,* and there can be no gift of self without an act of love.

Furthermore, the most natural disposition for mother and child to have toward one another is love; and from this flow all the other sentiments — thoughtfulness, kindness, self-sacrifice, gratitude, etc.

How could we call ourselves Mary's children if we would not foster filial love for her? To bring our hearts into loving conformity with our heavenly Mother's Heart — this should be the greatest and happiest task of our Marian devotion. Our sweet Mother says to us, *"Son, give me thy heart."* (Pr 23:26). "My Mother is playful," St. Joseph of Cupertino said jestingly. "If I bring her flowers, she tells me she does not want them. Then I ask her, 'Mother, what do you want, then" And she says, 'Your heart, only your heart satisfies me.'"

Along with acts that venerate her and our efforts to imitate her, then, we should give Mary our heart, that it may be like a chariot of fire in which veneration and imitation are both transported.

Reflect that if *"God… hath first loved us"* (I Jn 4:10), Our Lady, too, first loved us when she gave us — along with her answer, *"Be it done unto me according to thy word"* — her consent to be our Mother — a Mother who would have all the sorrows and all the treasures of grace entrusted to her as Mediatrix and Dispenser of divine favors.

Moreover, she does not fail to give herself wholly to us, even at times visibly renewing her immense mercy and her motherly care for us ungrateful and needy children. La Salette, Lourdes, Fatima, Syracuse

(Sicily), are places in which Our Lady made her love perceptible to the senses in order that by repeated efforts she might touch our hearts.

How have we responded and how are we responding to this great love? It is true that we all consider ourselves and call ourselves devoted clients of Our Lady; but what is the quality of the love in our Marian devotion?

Love and knowledge

Love requires first of all that we know the person who is loved. Hence we must instruct ourselves about Our Lady, otherwise we would offer her only a sentimental, blind love.

The better we know Our Lady, the more our love for her grows. The more we desire to love Our Lady, the more we should feel the need of delving into her mystery, of knowing her wonders, of discovering her heavenly charm.

It has always been a concern of the Magisterium of the Church to make Our Lady known, so that the love of her clients might be an enlightened love. Pope Paul VI's great Apostolic Exhortation, *The Cult of the Blessed Virgin*, serves to render more glorious and intelligible the knowledge of Our Lady in the liturgy and in the piety of the faithful.

Knowledge of Our Lady is especially gained *on our knees,* said St. Maximilian M. Kolbe; that is, with humble prayer. The saints prayed unwearyingly in order to obtain this gift of wisdom from the Holy Spirit.

But we also have the holy Doctors who studied and wrote to instruct the faithful, and left us masterpieces on Our Lady. We may mention St. John Damascene, St. Bernard, St. Bonaventure, St. Bernadine of Siena, St. Antoninus, St. Thomas of Villanova, St. Lawrence of Brindisi, St. Anthony M. Claret, etc. But there are above all two Marian works, St. Louis Grignion Montfort's *True Devotion to Mary*, and St. Alphonsus Liguori's *Glories of Mary*, that have cultivated an enlightened and strong Marian devotion in the souls of a number of generations. All the saints have learned from the master-teachers of the Church how to make their love for Our Lady something that sheds light and warmth.

St. Gemma Galgani read all the books she could obtain on Our Lady, and passed them on to others, urging them to read them too. She assisted at Marian functions during the months dedicated to Mary and during novenas in Mary's honor, and listened to the sermons and Marian instructions.

St. Dominic Savio used to read many things on Mary, including accounts of current Marian events and little episodes about her, in order to tell them later to his companions.

And what do we do? Would it be very costly for us to give just fifteen minutes to reading and meditating on Our Lady? It would be a matter of spending a quarter of an hour in company with our heavenly Mother. Alas! Should we have to be begged to do this?

Consider something that St. Gabriel of Our Lady of Sorrows wrote, who was a true lover of Our Lady: "I would not exchange a quarter of an hour spent in blessed Mary's company — who is our consolation, our portion, and our hope — for a year, or as much time as you like, in theaters and at worldly entertainments."

Love and union

The strongest demand of love is that we encounter, that we be near, that we be *united* to the one we love. By its very nature love unites. God is One because He is Love. Mother and child, husband and wife, brethren, friends — as long as they love one another they feel a bond of unity. Love is their bond of unity. If love grows cold, the bond of unity breaks down. It is all in proportion. The greater the love, the stronger the bond that unites. There can be no true love without true concord that makes for unity.

Jesus loves us all with an infinite Love. Hence He wants to become *"one"* with us and wants to make us one with Him. *"He that eateth My Flesh and drinketh My Blood abideth in Me: and I in him"* (Jn 6:57). One abides in the other. There is a fusion.

Therefore every true client of Mary should feel a spontaneous, natural need to love Our Lady by striving to always live united to her; just as a baby has a spontaneous urge to be near its mother and can do nothing without her, and grieves at her absence.

This is the way it was with the saints.

The Little Flower, St. Thérèse, used to say that she wanted to spend her "daytime of life hidden with Jesus under Mary's mantle." And even from babyhood, her life must have been taken up with thoughts on Our Lady if, after she was taken to visit Paris, the only thing she remembered of that wonderful city was the church of *Our Lady of Victories*.

That great devotee of Mary, St. Louis Grignion de Montfort, said of himself that he had been "predestined to dwell in Mary," and he attained such a degree of union with Our Lady that he came to continually enjoy her presence. At the end of his life he asked that his heart be buried under Mary's altar as an expression of his inseparable bond of love with his heavenly Queen.

When St. Gemma Galgani lost her mother at the age of seven, she entrusted herself to Our Lady: "From now on Our Lady will be my Mother." The bond of love between the heavenly Mother and her daughter took on an extraordinary sweetness. Our Lady made visible visits to the little Saint, and would caress her, kiss her, and hold her in her arms. She used to press this beloved daughter to her Heart, a daughter who later became a voluntary victim soul and suffered the stigmata for the salvation of souls.

St. Anthony M. Claret lived habitually so engrossed in Our Lady that once, when writing a letter, he headed it "Maria, March 3, 1866," instead of "Madrid…"

St. Maximilian M. Kolbe leaves us another extraordinary example of a life lived in a union of love with the Immaculate Virgin, his *dear Mother*. In his fervor he could not stop thinking about his great Queen. The Immaculate became his *fixed idea,* and he lived, suffered, and died for this *lovable and freely chosen fixed idea: the Immaculate.*

St. Pio of Pietrelcina became famous for the enormous number of Rosaries he recited day and night — about a hundred, five decades each. He always lived a life of union and contact with his sweet Mother. From the age of five, little Francis Forgione (his name before becoming a friar) enjoyed the visible presence of Our Lady. Her heavenly visits to him had such naturalness that, for a long time, he thought this experience was something common with others. Once after Francis had told his spiritual director about it, he asked the priest, "And do you not see Our Lady?" When he got a negative answer, Francis remarked, "You say that because you are humble." But humility had nothing to do with it. Francis alone was enjoying that presence of Mary, which was a sign of his profound union with her.

But a constant atmosphere of love can be found in all the saints, which nourished their bond with Our Lady; for some, the presence of Mary was a special, extraordinary grace, as happened with St. John Damascene, St. Matilda, St. Bridget, St. John Eudes, St. Margaret Mary Alacoque, St. Charles of Sezze, St. Veronica Giuliani, St. Alphonsus Liguori, and the holy Curé of Ars.

But it is of more interest to us to know the specific *acts of love* by which the saints always lived united to the heavenly Mother. Here is where all the saints have been our great masters, imitating Jesus who first began to do and then to teach (cf. Acts 1:1).

Love and acts of love

Marian prayer was the most productive source of those acts of love by which the saints kept united to Our Lady.

Prayers well said to the Blessed Virgin — with supplications, devotions, Rosaries, ejaculations, daily adorned their souls and their occupations — from their morning rising to the last blessing received at bedtime.

What has imbued the lives of Mary's true clients with Marian prayer has been especially the *Little Office of the Blessed Virgin*, so dear to many saints and, even more so, the holy Rosary. These have kept Our Lady's clients in constant union with her.

Marian prayer consists simply in this: meeting her, speaking with her, and being *united with her*.

But in this prayer-life, Mary's true clients ought to take care to shun above all anything displeasing to their sweet Mother; and that would be any sin, great or small. It would be simply absurd for us to want to love her or think we love her, while we are offending her.

Moreover, Mary's true client must bring Mary into all his affairs; he must depend on her in making his every choice, and must entrust to her the execution of every task, even the smallest. When St. Aloysius Gonzaga had to prepare the refectory for a meal, he used to say with ingenuous faith, "Let us go set the table for Jesus and Mary." The Saint brought Our Lady even into his simplest chores. Certainly all our chores are of interest to such a fond Mother. Nothing is a matter of indifference to her motherly love, which knows no cold reserve, and wants to endow all our actions with supernatural merit and beauty.

This is why the saints started off their day with a morning offering to Our Lady. The holy Curé of Ars, St. John Vianney, had the pleasing saying that every morning we should do as a baby does who, as soon as he wakes up, looks about from his crib for his mother.

Then, during the course of the day, the saints would not fail to call on Our Lady often. Love demanded this. For example, read this resolution of Bl. Contardo Ferrini:

"Every day after my visit to Jesus I will make a visit to Mary, whom I will often call to mind during the day... I will love holy purity, entrusting myself often to Mary... Before every conversation I will commit myself to her care with a Hail Mary. I will do the same before meals. Every day I will say the Rosary, and at noon, the Angelus. And every hour, when possible, I will pray a Hail Mary and make a spiritual communion."

How wonderful! And let us not forget that Bl. Contardo was a layman and a university professor. Who would be unable to imitate him? Why, then, not make our own good resolutions too?

If only we were to love…

Love and important activities

Especially in their more important activities, the devotees of Mary cannot overlook putting themselves in Mary's company, uniting themselves to Our Lady in order to act in her and with her.

As for assisting at holy Mass, for example, St. Pio of Pietrelcina recommended participating in it by keeping the Blessed Virgin company at the foot of the Cross. Hence he used to try to celebrate the Mass of the Immaculate Conception as often as the rubrical laws permitted. One time he sent for the liturgical calendar in order to know what days he could celebrate the votive Mass of the Immaculate Conception. St. Lawrence of Brindisi and Bl. Stephen Bellesini did the same. A Saint who reached an extraordinary union with Mary when he celebrated holy Mass was St. Cajetan. People said of him that, at his Masses, Our Lady herself seemed to be the celebrant.

During the first days of her new Congregation, St. Louise de Marillac had her small group of country girls assembled in her home. At the start of their meeting, she turned their attention to a statue of Our Lady, declaring her to be the one on whom she was relying. St. Angela Merici did likewise.

When St. Alphonsus Liguori was leaving the world to give himself to God, he went to Our Lady's statue and, laying his sword at her feet, he consecrated himself entirely to her.

St. Frances Xavier Cabrini crossed the ocean nineteen times. Twice during raging storms she sailed along the Pacific coast and three times among the shores of the Atlantic. Each time, she started and ended her voyages with the Rosary in her hand.

When St. Pius X was elected Pope, he entrusted his pontificate to Our Lady and dedicated his first encyclical letter to her.

St. Bartholomew Capitanio wrote out his resolutions for a holy life and, then, in the following prayer, entrusted to Our Lady what he had written: "Dear Mother, I entrust this writing to you. Be you the one who makes me fulfill it."

When he was developing his project of the great *City of the Immaculate,* St. Maximilian M. Kolbe placed a statue of the Immaculate on an estate in Poland that was not yet his own. Then, because of unexpected developments, the owner decided not to grant him the land after all, and suggested that the statue be taken away. But the Saint replied with simplicity that the statue ought to remain there "at least to show that just once Our Lady had failed in her promises." The owner was touched by this reply, reconsidered, and granted the whole estate to St. Maximilian for his project.

St. Thérèse, the Little Flower, offered herself to be a "victim to merciful Love" through Mary's hands. Before writing her Story of a Soul (her autobiography), she knelt before Our Lady and begged her to take her by the hand "so that not even a line written by me will not be acceptable to you." Also, St. Catherine of Siena chose to begin her celebrated *Dialogues* on *Mary's day*, namely, Saturday.

On his wedding day, the Servant of God, Vico Necchi, instead of going on a honeymoon, made a pilgrimage to Lourdes to entrust to Our Lady the new family that he was starting.

When we entrust everything to our sweet Mother, nothing but profit comes of it — in virtue, in grace, in love.

Love and virginity

Here is a delicate point: Commonly, religious sisters have lovingly sought to arrange that the joyful event of their consecration to the heavenly Bridegroom occur on a day dear to Mary. What an identity there is between virginity and Mary Most Holy! Is not Our Lady the true Virgin, the perfect Virgin, who is forever and preeminently a Virgin? Innocent and lovely with a spotless fragrance, Our Lady's spiritual and bodily virginity has the dazzling brilliance of the sun. All good virgins bear a ray of that dazzling brightness within them, which tends to refashion them into a likeness of the Blessed Virgin. This is why, almost by instinct, they love to give themselves to Jesus with Mary and through Mary, and prefer days that are especially dear to her so as to feel more united to her.

Every year, St. Teresa of Jesus renewed religious vows with her daughters on the day of *Mary's Nativity* (September 8th) and on the day of *Mary's Presentation in the Temple* (November 21st).

St. Margaret Mary Alacoque chose to enter the convent on a Saturday, the weekday dedicated to Mary.

The life of St. Thérèse of Lisieux has several Marian anniversaries: Her entry into Carmel was on the feast of the *Annunciation*; she became a spouse of Jesus on the feast of *Mary's Nativity*; she received holy Viaticum on the feast of *Our Lady of Mt. Carmel*.

St. Gemma Galgani had the good fortune of taking her vow of virginity on December 8th, the Solemnity of the *Immaculate Conception*, and she made her flight to paradise on Holy Saturday, 1903. Her Beatification and Canonization both occurred during the month of May.

St. Bertilla Boscardin received the religious habit on the feast of the *Purity of Mary*, and made her profession on the solemnity of the *Immaculate Conception*.

To combine one's consecration to virginity with the Blessed Virgin's feasts goes into the refinements of love. True devotion to Our Lady makes love ever more delicate, even to the sweetest refinement. Oh, what disarming resourcefulness and tenderness are often evident! This is the virginal tenderness of Our Lady which is so imprinted in the pure hearts of these virgins. It so sweetens their characters that, as St. Thérèse of Lisieux said, every movement of their hearts "buds forth charity."

Love and sacrifice

There is no surer proof of true love than self-sacrifice. There is no greater and purer love than that which moves one to sacrifice himself for the one he loves. Jesus said, *"Greater love than this no man hath, that a man lay down his life for his friends"* (Jn 15:13).

In order to be certain about love, it has to be tested by sacrifice; otherwise we are likely to be deluded.

But there is more. True love reaches the point of not being able to operate without sacrifice: it needs sacrifice. It craves it and seeks it. "Let me either suffer or die," was the plea of St. Teresa of Avila to Jesus.

Love for Our Lady, too, is evaluated on the scale of sacrifice. If one knows how to sacrifice himself for her, there can be no doubt about the purity of his love.

Among the aints, sacrifice has always played a dominant role. They felt a need to nourish their love for Our Lady with sacrifice. One can say of each of them what was said of St. Catherine Labouré: "She lived with a continual desire to suffer for her love."

For example, St. Joseph Cafasso devised a system of devout pledges, a special Rosary of pledges, that he himself called his "burden." It was composed of fifty small mortifications to be offered to Our Lady. He loved to prepare for Mary's feasts and observe the month of May in this manner, thereby enriching his love with daily, voluntary sacrifices.

Bl. Fortunata Viti prepared for Our Lady's feasts by wearing a cilice for an hour a day, or by taking the discipline for several minutes, and she mortified her palate by mixing ashes into her soup.

Before the feast of the Assumption, St. Paul of the Cross devised for himself a *Lent for the Assumption*, during which he fasted rigorously, abstained from fruit, and prayed the complete Rosary every day. Once the Saint became ill during one of these Lents and completely lost his appetite. The Brother infirmarian was worried, and managed to obtain an apple for him, hoping to get him to eat it. The Saint would have liked to eat it, but did not want to touch it because it was during Our Lady's Lent. The Brother insisted that he at least taste it, but the Saint excused himself by saying, "We are in Our Lady's Lent. Let us make an offering of it to her."

Practices that have been characteristic and common with the saints, include a fervent preparation for Our

Lady's feasts and a dedication of every Saturday to Mary, hallowing it by a fast or by abstaining from meat (or from fruit, or from desserts and other sweets). The Saints who so honored Mary include St. Charles Borromeo, St. Francis de Sales, St. Lawrence of Brindisi, St. Catherine of Siena, Bl. Anna M. Taigi. We venture to say that the number of Saints one might include would almost be incalculable.

Love without respite

The saints at times performed extraordinary acts of sacrifice for their heavenly Queen, acts that fill us with awe and admiration. St. Veronica Giuliani put Mary's name on her breast with a red-hot iron. St. Gabriel of Our Lady of Sorrows wanted to do the same, but his superiors would not give permission; nor could he write with his own blood the *"Marian creed,"* which he always wore hanging over his heart. Bl. Theofane Venard, on the other hand, did write an act of consecration to Our Lady in his own blood.

But no less heroic than these extraordinary acts is a steadfast love nourished by little, unnoticed sacrifices. Every day St. Dominic Savio (as St. John Bosco reports) offered some mortification to the Blessed Virgin. St. Gabriel of Our Lady of Sorrows wrote out this resolution: "Not a day will pass me by without my offering a garland of virtues practiced to crown the head of my Virgin Mother."

The Servant of God Felicita Rossi often kissed the ground when no one was looking. Someone discovered it and asked for the reason. She answered, "What did Our Lady say to Bernadette? She said to kiss the ground for sinners." She was generously doing just that.

St. Bernadette, when she was sick and coughing violently, once cried out, "Open up my lungs!" But when someone wanted to have her drink some of the miraculous water from the Lourdes grotto she said, "The spring is not for me. Our Lady wills that I might suffer."

Who can forget the beautiful examples of sacrifice left us by the three little shepherds of Fatima? They willingly suffered thirst, hunger, and heat. They looked for penance, and this led them to whip their legs with prickly bush-stems and wear a rough cord next to their skin, tightened about the waist. They did all this to console the Immaculate Heart of Mary and obtain the conversion of sinners.

A recent and glorious example is the life of St. Maximilian M. Kolbe. He let his life be consumed day by day as a sacrifice of love for the heavenly Mother's sake. He was not afraid to be considered a fool as he undertook ambitious projects to serve the Immaculate — projects that cost him dearly again and again when he had intermittent periods of hospitalization and became a victim and oblation on the altar of sacrifice. On one occasion, he was brought to see an exhibit held in Rome. Afterwards, someone asked him what had been of particularly interest to him. He gave this candid answer: "Nothing, nothing could have been of interest to me; I did not notice anything at all. I advance along the way for the Immaculate." His love for the Immaculate truly knew no rest and was always *advancing*.

Love and compassion

Another essential characteristic of love is the sharing in the pains of the one loved. It may be true that one can be indifferent to the joys of the beloved, but one cannot lack compassion for the beloved in his sufferings.

We should never forget that when Jesus gave us Our Lady as Mother, it was not on a festive occasion, but on Calvary at the very hour when she was plunged in a sea of grief, when she was *"bringing forth children in sorrow"* (cf. Gen 3:16). Making reference to His sorrowing Mother, Jesus repeats anew to each of us His words to St. John the Evangelist, *"Behold, thy Mother"* (Jn 19:27).

Therefore Mary's true devotees have always loved the devotion to her Sorrows. It is fitting here to recall some examples of the saints which will spur us on towards greater love for the Sorrowful Mother.

St. Anthony Pucci was a great lover and apostle of the Sorrowful Virgin. He used to speak of her in a tender, moving way, and would pass out holy cards with her image wherever he could, even on a sailing vessel — posting them on the very sails and cabin doors. He persuaded people to recite the special Rosary called the Crown of the Seven Sorrows, and he promoted the practice of celebrating September as the month dedicated to the Sorrowful Mother.

Another great client of the Sorrowful Mother was St. Paul of the Cross. The mere thought of the grief-stricken Mother would often move him to tears. He used to speak of her Sorrows by using an excellent comparison: "Mary's Sorrows are like the waters of the Mediterranean, which cast themselves into the boundless ocean of Jesus' Passion."

St. Gabriel of Our Lady of Sorrows, a spiritual son of St. Paul of the Cross and a fervent devotee of Mary's Sorrows, wrote that "Mary's Sorrows are my Paradise." It was especially during Holy Week and during the whole month of September that he would spend much time in devout meditation on the *Sorrows of the beloved Mother*. A fellow friar wrote that "the mere sight of him so recollected throughout the day, or off in some corner of the choir to pray, would deeply move one's heart to compunction."

A final example is the seraphic St. Gemma Galgani, a true flower of the Passion who suffered crucifixion with Jesus; she was a favored daughter of the Sorrowful Mother. As a small child she received a little statue of Our Lady of Sorrows as a gift from her mother. When her mother died, St. Gemma consecrated herself as Mary's daughter, before this Madonna. From then on, her life was that of a victim soul, crucified with Jesus; and she kept inseparable company with the heavenly Mother.

"Mother, where are you?" she exclaimed in ecstasy. "You are always at the foot of Jesus' Cross… My dear Mother was crucified with Jesus and never regretted it… After this reflection I have resolved not to grumble any more… And tomorrow I want a favor from Our Lady; that is, that she give me a big, heavy cross…"

This is how the saints love. They are Mary's true clients.

And how do we respond? Is it perhaps not true that, with our kind of love, instead of wanting to offer sacrifices for Our Lady, we only seek to escape from all the troubles and sufferings of life? Is this true love?

Our Lady said to St. Bernadette, "I will not make you happy with the happiness of this world."

Our Lady's kind of love does not tend to worldly happiness, but to a happiness that is of Heaven. Let us sigh for that heavenly happiness and share the pains of this exile with our heavenly Mother who suffers for all her children who are still in exile.

"Make her loved"

There are two things that go together like fire and heat: loving Our Lady and making her loved. Heat naturally emerges from fire. Likewise, love for Our

Lady is spontaneously translated into the Marian apostolate.

The beautiful exhortation. "Love Our Lady and make her loved," was one of Padre Pio's favorite sayings, and in this respect he was a model. "Would that I had a very powerful voice," he said, "to invite sinners all over the world to love Our Lady."

His love for Our Lady was contagious. Who can count his spiritual children who learned from him to use the Rosary and say dozens of them daily? And how many Rosaries, holy medals, images and little statues he distributed to those who visited him!

Love moves people to speak of the one they love. We know that the Church's greatest orators and writers have spoken, written, and sung Our Lady's praises with tireless zeal and love. We may cite, for example, St. Ephrem, St. John Damascene, St. Bernard, St. Alphonsus Liguori. But there has not been a saint, nor will there ever be any true devotee of Mary who does not feel a need to share his love for Our Lady with others. In big ways or small, the true devotee does all that he can to accomplish this in accord with the inspirations and talents he has received.

There have been some who were able to found religious congregations and institutes in honor of the Blessed Virgin. This was done, for example, by St. Francis de Sales, St. Anthony Claret, St. John Bosco, Ven. William Chaminade, and many others.

Some had a special Marian mission to accomplish in behalf of all men. This includes, for example, St. Catherine Labouré, using the Miraculous Medal, and Sister Maria Lucia of Fatima, by means of devotion to the Immaculate Heart of Mary.

An outstanding example

St. Maximilian M. Kolbe, who is considered the greatest Marian apostle of the twentieth century, founded two unique *Cities of the Immaculate* as centers to promote the Marian apostolate throughout the world. The zeal of this apostle, who was willing to be called a *"fool for the Immaculate,"* showed itself in many ways, which included his great ambition to make every soul a "conquest of Mary Immaculate." He dreamed of a network of *Cities of the Immaculate* which would encircle the globe and flood it with Marian literature and Miraculous Medals, which would serve to bring devotion for Our Lady to every heart.

St. Maximilian founded the *Militia of the Immaculate* as a movement of Marian life and apostleship for those souls that want to consecrate themselves to the Immaculate as her *property* and want to engage in an active apostolate under her sweet rule — an apostolate that would use all — we stress the word *all* — legitimate means, old and new, present and future, little and great (e.g., the Miraculous Medal, the press, the theater, music, cultural movements, radio, television, cinema, and we may add telestar satellites and telecommunication networks). "Everything should be, first of all, for the service of the Immaculate," St. Maximilian M. Kolbe used to say.

In order to move souls to love Mary, St. Maximilian ventured to make great, self-effacing, personal sacrifices. He made exhausting journeys on missions that seemed foolish, so much so that a saying circulated that he wanted to "make a trip to the moon on a hoe." But he went ahead undaunted, carrying on with hard work and privation: fainting spells on the train, having to celebrate Mass while supported by two friars, repeatedly coughing up blood, becoming emaciated, even proving himself unpopular with certain persons. He never stopped! His love for the Immaculate would not let him rest from his feverish activity. There was a time in Japan when people, upon seeing his tireless activity, thought he must be part of what they called the "myth of immortality."

One time, when he was traveling on the feast of the Holy Name of Mary, September 12, 1932, he had the inspiration to write a letter to Our Lady, as from a son to his mother. It was to convey to Our Lady his good wishes on the occasion of her feast day. At the end he signed his affectionate letter "Fr. Maximilian M. Kolbe, far from home, between Saigon and Hong Kong, on a rough sea and in burning heat — all for you, O Mary!"

He was tireless and daring, and when someone told him to lighten up a little, he answered smilingly,

"I have no time to rest here below. I will take my rest in Paradise." This is the way of true love.

Serve her in every way

The task of making Our Lady loved has a limitless field of operation. There is a place for everyone. Everywhere there are things to do, and all kinds of things.

A boy like a St. Dominic Savio is able to start a small *Association of the Immaculate* among his schoolmates. A humble Sister like St. Catherine Labouré starts the *Daughters of Mary*, which is flourishing almost everywhere in the world.

St. Aloysius Gonzaga, St. Gabriel of Our Lady of Sorrows, St. Bernadette, St. Gemma Galgani, profited by every opportunity to introduce Our Lady into people's lives. Both by word and example they strove to persuade souls to love her. St. Gabriel in particular has left us a deeply moving example. Among his fellow religious he was called "promoter of devotion to Mary." Among his relatives and acquaintances outside his monastery, he promoted devotion to Our Lady in various forms, like the observance of May and October as months dedicated to Mary, the daily recitation of the holy Rosary, the reading of Marian books, the wearing of the Carmelite scapular, recitation of the Crown of the Seven Sorrows. A year before his death he made a vow that he would always and everywhere spread devotion to Our Lady.

Even as a child St. Thérèse of Lisieux was an apostle of the Miraculous Medal. Later she wrote, "If I had only been a priest, oh, how much I would have spoken in behalf of Our Lady!"

This desire of St. Thérèse reminds us of the fervent love with which holy priests have brought Our Lady to souls. St. Peter Canisius, besides spreading knowledge of Our Lady by his writings, worked as an unwearying apostle to make her loved. He tirelessly journeyed about founding Marian societies for the laity, both young and old, getting them to develop the practice of reciting the holy Rosary fervently and daily. When, as an old man, he hobbled about the streets of Freiburg with his cane, crowds of men, women and children used to gather around him to ask his blessing. The Saint gladly blessed them, but always had them promise to have devotion to Our Lady and to recite the holy Rosary every day.

Every Saturday without fail, St. Alphonsus Liguori used to preach about the glories of Mary, and he had a wonderful way of drawing souls to the feet of the *divine Mary*.[6]

St. John Vianney, the Curé of Ars, could not hide the intense love that moved him when he gave instructions to the people about Our Lady. He has left

6 *Translator's note:* Obviously St. Alphonsus is *not* saying that Mary is God, but that she belongs entirely to God (e.g. divine worship means the worship *of God*, and not that worship is God), that she is entirely divinized and God-like, yet remaining forever a humble creature.

us his *Marian catechisms* which are full of charm and light, and glow with tender affection for Our Lady.

St. Joseph Cafasso distributed thousands of little holy cards of Our Lady free of charge. He often spoke to his penitents about devotion to Mary and moved them to cultivate it. As much as he could, he circulated copies of St. Alphonsus' book *The Glories of Mary*, in order to instill in people a devotion to Our Lady which would be enlightening and doctrinally solid.

Let us, too, use all our energies and every means at hand to make Our Lady loved everywhere.

We should bear in mind that the Marian apostolate offers a sure pledge of Paradise to its apostles and to those who heed them. In her Liturgy, the Church has Our Lady say, *"They that explain me shall have life everlasting"* (Ec 24:31). Does this not console us? Furthermore, we should realize that when we succeed in getting someone to love Our Lady, we have gained his salvation. When Our Lady enters a heart, she always brings Jesus our Savior. She is always Jesus' Mother; it is always she who begets Jesus in all the hearts that receive her. For this reason, St. Maximilian Kolbe used to say that we must "introduce the Immaculate Mother to all hearts so that, once she enters within them, she may take possession of them, bring sweet Jesus there, and make Him grow to the perfect age."

IMITATING OUR LADY

Imitation is a daughter of love. It consists in making our actions agree with those of the one we love. He who loves, imitates. It is the nature of love to unite, to render as one. Love is complete and perfect once it has made lovers completely one, even their actions, not allowing any differences that hinder unity. For this reason, love cannot exist without imitation; otherwise there would be no unity of wills.

Imitation, then, is love's demeanor and a true expression of love's fruitfulness. If we say it is love's daughter, we mean that wherever imitation is, love is, and wherever imitation is not, love is not. And where imitation reaches its peak, love is at its peak.

St. Pius X upheld this teaching when he said, "If anyone wishes (and who should not so wish?) that his devotion to the Virgin be complete and perfect in every respect, then it is necessary that he strive by every effort to imitate her example."

Imitation of Mary and sanctity

Imitation of Mary is the element that clearly and precisely distinguishes a holy person's devotion to

Our Lady from that of one who is not holy. A little reflection suffices to make this clear.

The saint loves Our Lady by perfectly imitating her virtues, and he is a saint by reason of this imitation. But we, instead, love Our Lady with a love that very imperfectly imitates her virtues, or is content with pious desires. There we are always mediocre, with a half-hearted devotion that is in danger of becoming no more than "a barren and passing sentimentalism," and of degenerating into "a kind of vain credulity," as the Second Vatican Council said (Lumen Gentium, n. 67).

It is wrong, then, to put the blame on Marian devotion when it is not bearing fruit and leaves us always the same. Pius XII admonishes, "Do not forget that in order for devotion to Our Lady to be recognizable as true and solid and hence productive of precious fruit and abundant grace, one must nourish it by imitating the life of her whom one wants to honor." Pope Paul VI often emphasized the fact that true Marian devotion requires the imitation of Mary's virtues: "The sons and daughters will be adorned with these virtues of their Mother, if, with unwavering resolution, they consider her example in order to reproduce it in their lives."

This has always been the Church's teaching which aims for solidity and moves towards the concrete: she desires works, she desires virtues. Devotion to Our Lady ought to lead every soul to become an image of

Mary, the person dearest to God, because she is the one most like Jesus.

Now if we want to evaluate the vitality and strength of our devotion to Mary, it is enough to examine how well we imitate Mary. If we see in ourselves a sincere and constant effort to imitate Our Lady's virtues, then our Marian devotion is true "in every respect," as St. Pius X assures us. This follows St. Augustine's teaching that "true devotion consists in imitating the virtues of those whom we love."

We should aim at imitation, therefore. Only then are we sure of having a solid foundation. Devotion to Our Lady is like a garden that should yield flowers of great beauty, flowers of Marian virtue. But what is the condition of our garden? Is it without flowers?

Let us look seriously into the matter, without pretence or superficiality. Let us compare ourselves with the saints. Let us evaluate our scant love in the light of their rich, overflowing love. Let us humble ourselves, and learn from them how to imitate her who "shines forth as a model of virtue to the whole community of the elect." (*Lumen Gentium*, n. 65).

"How would Our Lady do this?"

One method, as simple as it is essential, of imitating all Our Lady's virtues is asking ourselves, whenever we would do anything, "How would Our Lady do this in my place?" Anyone can put this question to himself, and he would not have to wait long for results.

St. Catherine Labouré, so loved by Mary, had this rule of life: "I will take Mary as my model at the start of my actions and I will reflect how she would do the task that I am about to do."

In her great devotion to Our Lady, St. Thérèse of Lisieux drew up a plan of life to completely "follow the footsteps of Mary." Considering herself as a little child, she commented, "Ordinarily little children resemble their mother."

St. Anthony Mary Claret, the great apostle of the Rosary and of Mary's Heart during the 19th century, was able to say that he had so lived as to always attentively and keenly maintain a profound union with Mary — a union whereby he depended on her in everything and for everything. When he was appointed Archbishop of Cuba, he wrote this program for his life: "My way of governing will be what Our Lady inspires... For holy Mary is my Mother, my Instructor, my Director..."

Another great Servant of God, Father Chautard, followed the same simple way, and used to ask himself before every undertaking, "How would Our Lady do this in my place?" He was endeavoring to live *under Mary's surveillance,* seeking as far as possible to make his view *coincide* with hers, in order to know what to do and how to act in the way most pleasing to her.

Let us remember that there is no more authentic proof of reverence and love than imitation. The disciple esteems and loves his master in the measure that he tries to become like him.

Hence St. Teresa of Avila used to repeat to her Sisters that the best way to honor Our Lady is to imitate her virtues. St. Stanislaus Kostka, St. Aloysius Gonzaga, St. Veronica Giuliani, St. Gabriel of Our Lady of Sorrows, gave glory to Our Lady by lovingly studying her virtues in order to reproduce them in their every day lives. They were not satisfied with feeling ardent desires, rendering sweet sighs and shedding tears (which seem so important to us), but they eagerly sought after the virtues that would fashion their souls into perfect likenesses of Mary's beauty.

St. Lucy Filippini was described as a "faithful copy" of Mary, especially in her charity, humility, purity, and patience. And other *faithful copies* of Our Lady were St. Catherine, St. Rose, St. Bernadette, St. Thérèse of Lisieux, St. Gemma, with those other holy women in whom shone the glorious beauty of Mary's virginity, charity, faith, hope, humility, fortitude, and self-sacrifice.

The Servant of God, Don Placid Baccher, spent his life in the city of Naples. He was a holy priest, and was so very devoted to Mary that people described him as "entirely Our Lady's priest entirely." What a beautiful tribute! And so it should be for all true devotees of Our Lady. This description has fitted all the saints since the more holy they became, the more they necessarily became likenesses of her who "is most like to Christ" (Dante).

In every virtue

St. Louis Grignion de Montfort wrote that "true devotion to the holy Virgin... leads a soul to avoid sin and imitate the holy Virgin's virtues, and in a special way her deep humility, her lively faith, her blind obedience, her continual prayer, her universal mortification, her heavenly purity, her ardent charity, her heroic patience, her angelic sweetness and her heavenly wisdom." What a lovely array of virtues is seen in this all-heavenly creature!

In his exhortation, *The Cult of the Blessed Virgin*, Pope Paul VI gives an almost identical list of Mary's virtues, which he recommends for our imitation.

Our Lady "is the model for the whole Church," says St. Augustine; and she is the model of all virtues, not just a few, and not some more than others. She presents to us the perfection of every virtue — a perfection which we cannot equal, but can love; which is sublime and awesome, yet imitable. *"In me is all hope of life and of virtue"* (Ec 24:25), Mary tells us with the words of the Prophet, as used in the sacred Liturgy. And let not the lofty perfection of her virtues frighten us. Our Lord Himself told us, *"Learn of Me"* (Mt 11:29), and He imposed on us the duty of striving to become *"perfect as the Father in Heaven is perfect"* (Mt 5:48).

Together with Jesus, Our Lady can tell us, *"I have given you an example, that as I have done…, so you do also"* (Jn 13:15). And her example is closer to us, more to our measure, rendered lovable by the brightness of grace, sweetened according to the unique ways of motherly tenderness. Therefore, her virtues are sublime, awe-inspiring and sweet at the same time. They are not frightening. On the contrary, they are attractive on account of the simplicity with which she practiced them in an extremely humble and ordinary life.

Let us model ourselves after her, therefore. She is the perfect model of the human person raised by grace. By imitating her, we come to share in her heavenly perfection. This depends only on us — on our consent. Let us therefore proceed at once in this holy undertaking! Let us put into practice the beautiful exhortations that the great Bishop Bossuet gave to listeners of his sermons: "Produce a holy image for the Queen of Heaven. May you yourselves be that image. Everyone is the painter and the sculptor of his own life. Fashion your lives then after the holy Virgin and may you be faithful copies of that perfect original."

Her wonderful faith

Among her virtues, Our Lady's faith shines most splendidly in Heaven. After having heard and understood the message of the Angel, she believed, and spoke her *"fiat"* (*"Be it done unto me according to thy word"* Lk 1:38), her acceptance of things which, humanly speaking, were unthinkable: to believe in the Incarnation of the Divine Word, the Son of God; to become herself the Mother of God; to conceive and give birth in a virginal manner to the Word of God made man in her immaculate body by the operation of the Holy Spirit, and become the Mother, Coredemptrix and Mediatrix of the human race (cf. Lk 1:26–38).

Without arguing, Our Lady believed all these supernatural realities. St. Elizabeth thus declared under divine impulse, *"Blessed art thou who hast believed!"* (Lk 1:45). She believed blindly, and found herself full of God. The Word filled her virginal womb, and she was able to adore God enclosed within herself. She adored Him in her arms at the grotto in Bethlehem. She adored Him throughout His hidden life in Nazareth. She adored Him on the Cross. She adored Him under the appearances of bread and wine.

To what depths did her faith not reach? It would be useless to try to measure it. No saint, no creature will ever be able to match her example of superhuman faith, which triumphantly passed every test of suffering.

In imitation of the Mother of God, true clients of Mary ought to live a life of faith with unconquerable fortitude, never drawing back in the face of trial and suffering.

Let us consider the wonderful example of St. Maximilian M. Kolbe.

When the Saint had been arrested, he was shut in the notorious prison at Warsaw called Pawiak. One day a German official, who was fiercer than all the others, made an inspection of the prisoners. He entered the cell which the Saint shared with two others, and on seeing Kolbe in the garb of a friar, he went into a rage. He immediately walked up to Kolbe, took hold of the Crucifix on the Rosary hanging from his side, and, yanking it, he cried in a hostile tone, "And you believe in this?"

"Indeed I do believe in it!" Kolbe replied tranquilly.

The officer at once gave Kolbe a brutal blow in the face. Then two more times, the same question, the same answer, the same violent blow. His cellmates were struck with horror and enraged, but could do nothing. When the officer had left, it was St. Maximilian who tried to pacify the rage of his friends, remarking, "Now, now! This is just a small matter. Anyway, everything is offered to Our Blessed Mother."

Poverty and prayer

What we have said about Our Lady's faith, we can say likewise about all her other virtues. But then the discussion of them would never end. Besides, the essential thing is to be convinced that the saints have found in the Mother of God a most clear mirror of their every virtue — and for us to also find our own.

St. Francis of Assisi, fond spouse of Lady Poverty, could not reflect on the Blessed Virgin's poverty without himself being deeply moved. Once, at table, a friar made mention of Our Lady's poverty in the cave at Bethlehem. St. Francis immediately felt his emotions surging, rose from his place, took his plate, and went to a place in a corner, where he broke out into tears of sweet affection over Mary's poverty.

It was the same way with St. Clare of Assisi, who presented "the poverty and humility of Our Lord Jesus Christ and of His holy Mother" as the model for her daughters to imitate in their very poor and needy convent.

Regarding poverty, we want to remember also St. Maximilian M. Kolbe, who would always put *poverty and the Immaculate* together considering them to be inseparable and calling them the pillars of his foundation. The poverty he practiced was truly admirable in which he lacked even certain necessities, such as shoes, a blanket, food. But he relished these privations for the glory of his Queen.

Regarding Mary's life of prayer, we can mention St. Teresa of Avila and all the convents of Carmel in which the holy Foundress of the reform wanted to see Our Lady's prayer-life at Nazareth faithfully copied. Theirs was to be a life that, in a real, inexpressible way, would be all *"hidden with Christ in God"* (Col 3:3).

St. Margaret Mary Alacoque gave special attention to imitating Our Lady during the more important moments of holy Mass. At the offertory, she would resolve to imitate Mary's obedience as was manifested in the mystery of the Presentation of Jesus in the temple. At the consecration, she endeavored to imitate Our Lady's sacrifice at the foot of the Cross on Calvary. At Communion time, she sought to emulate the love that Our Lady had when the Word became flesh within her virginal body.

Why can we not do likewise?

At San Giovanni Rotondo one used to have an idea of Our Lady's ceaseless prayer, by watching St. Pio of Pietrelcina as he prayed hour after hour in the choir, in his cell, in the garden, in the corridors, by day and by night, reciting about a hundred Rosaries. If a man could pray so much, what must have been the Mother of God's capacity for prayer?

Humility and virginity

As for humility and virginal chastity, it is well-nigh impossible to think of a saint who did not draw inspiration from Our Lady in the course of perfecting himself in these two wonderful virtues. The imitation of Mary's humility and purity is the imitation most often spoken of. Perhaps it is because they are two virtues so closely linked to one another and so naturally associated with Our Lady, that they seem to be copied from her, the perfect universal model for all of us.

It is certain that the great devotees of Our Lady have given special attention to these two virtues of hers and, in their turn, have become models of profound humility and radiant purity themselves.

St. Catherine Labouré, for example, favored by heavenly apparitions of the Immaculate Virgin who entrusted the Miraculous Medal to her, remained hidden away in her humility throughout her long life, and no one knew that she was the Sister involved in these heavenly apparitions.

We should be mindful also of St. Bernadette's humility, who wrote among her resolutions, "I will make my happiness consist in living my life forgotten by others." In another note she wrote, "A principal grace to ask for is to live a hidden life after the example of Jesus and Mary." She was greatly favored by the Immaculate; she was the seer who was full of innocence and was known everywhere. Yet there was no danger of her falling into vainglory about the apparitions she had experienced. One small incident reveals to us her deep modesty.

One day, after Lourdes had become a famous shrine (while the Saint remained out of public sight), someone showed her a picture postcard of Lourdes. The Saint looked at it, and then uttered a rather strange question, "What does one do with a broom?"

"Oh! What a question! One sweeps with it."

"And after you sweep, what happens to it?"

"It is returned to its place in a corner."

"Well, it is the same with me. The holy Virgin has made some use of me. Then she puts me back to my place in a hidden corner, and there I remain."

The imitation of Mary's virginity shines radiantly in all virgins consecrated to God. And in this way, oh! what lovely likenesses of the Blessed Virgin they become!

St. Gerard Majella felt a special respect for sisters precisely because, as he said, "they represent the Mother of God." And this special reverence is not so surprising when we think of St. Clare, St. Catherine, St. Margaret, St. Bernadette, the Little Flower, and all the holy sisters among the immense multitude of consecrated Virgins. Even outwardly they seem to resemble the Virgin in the purity of their features, in their long habits and their wide veils that hide them from creatures. No longer belonging to this wretched world, they almost seem like angels. In fact, virginity may be called angelical. It is a privileged gift that Jesus bestows on only a comparative few (Mt 19:11), which enables a person to anticipate on earth a condition of life belonging to Paradise (Mt 22:30). But the whole value of virginity derives from the Blessed Virgin. All pure virgins are indebted to Our Lady's spotless virginity for the great value of their treasure; that is, it comes from the time when God so loved virginity that He chose a Virgin, Mary, as His instrument for the Incarnation, taking His human life and birth from her ever-virginal body. *Virginity, 'angelicity', maternity* — these shine gloriously in Mary and reflect in every virgin chosen and favored by God.

Therefore pure virgins make up the preferred ranks in the Marian army. They are souls called to follow the Blessed Virgin to form her train, of which the Holy Spirit speaks by the mouth of the Prophet: *"After her shall virgins be brought"* (Ps 41:15). St. Ambrose has written some beautiful pages on this point. At the end of time, virgins will have the happy fortune, in company with the Blessed Virgin, to *"follow the Lamb whithersoever He goeth"* (Apoc 14:4). These brides of Christ always follow the heavenly Bridegroom, bound by an unbreakable tie of virginal love that even in this world savors of that joyful, ardent, full-blossomed love which, by remaining faithful, they will have in eternity.

Holy purity

Consecrated virginity is a *"pearl of great price"* (cf. Mt 13:45) and a *"hidden treasure"* (cf. Mt 13:44). God gives it only to favored souls whose love is total and exclusive (cf. I Cor 7:25–35). The virtue of purity, on the other hand, is a virtue for all, which all Christians must practice with their whole heart. *"Blessed are the pure of heart..."* (Mt 5:8).

Our Lady is the *Mother most pure* not only because of the immaculate virginity that always shone in her soul and her body, but also because of her heavenly modesty, her sweet reserve, her thorough mortification of the senses, which were always absorbed in Jesus, the perfect and total object of her love.

Now, how would it be possible to love Our Lady if one does not thoroughly practice this angelic virtue so dear to her heart? Even if impurity is not the worst sin, it is yet certainly repulsive to Our Lady in every respect. And the saints have had a sensitive conscience about this, loving Our Lady with an angelic purity that they preserved in their souls, in their senses, in their bodies.

St. Dominic Savio, from the time he was a child, used to pray to Our Lady in this manner, "O my Mother, I want always to be your little child. Obtain for me that I may die rather than commit a sin against the virtue of modesty."

This boy was truly remarkable in maintaining custody of the senses, especially in mortifying his eyes. One time when he crossed a public square where sports activities were taking place, a companion saw St. Dominic keeping his eyes cast down, and asked him, "Dominic, why do you go with your eyes cast down, instead of watching the games?"

The Saint answered, "I want to keep my eyes pure to behold Our Lady in Paradise."

Such is the way of love. And one certainly cannot love Our Lady when he lets his eyes freely gaze at obscene objects, read unchaste literature, peer curiously at immodest sights. There can be no love for Our Lady on the part of all those women, young or old, who follow indecent fashions, becoming unhappy instruments of Satan *to arouse the lust of men, thus "drawn to their death"* (Pr 7:22). What a tragedy!

But a greater tragedy is the sea of filth that is flooding society in the form of bad movies and impure theatrical performances, depraved publications, scandalous bathing resorts and places of amusement, sexual perversions of all kinds and, notably, the scandal of wicked laws approving divorce, artificial birth control, and abortion. Everything seems to cater to man's tainted flesh. Alas for humanity!

A little girl of seven, Bl. Jacinta of Fatima, after being instructed by Our Lady, was able to tell all the world that, "The sins that send most souls to hell are the sins of impurity." The greatest grief afflicting Our Lady comes from sins of impurity, defiling souls and bodies all over the world and drawing down on mankind the great punishment of *"the anger of God"* (Eph 5:3-6).

Who will console Our Lady in this sorrow, if not her devout clients? It is they who must love Our Lady with a pure heart, a clean soul, and a chaste body, according to God's will for every state of life. The virginal fragrance of Our Lady's love for us ought to make us careful and conscientious to return it with a love and devotion imbued with uncompromised chastity.

Charity, the royal virtue

"By this shall all men know that you are my disciples, if you have love one for another" (Jn 13:35). An aim not only of every saint, but of certain entire religious orders and religious institutes has been to imitate Our Lady in this love for our brother.

Our Lady's charity, which was manifested as she went to visit St. Elizabeth, carrying Jesus to sanctify John the Baptist, so deeply moved, for example, Brother Charles De Foucauld, that he sought to imitate her by going among the Tuareg people in the Sahara in order to bring the Eucharistic Jesus into their midst.

And all the congregations or institutes that are inspired by the mystery of the Visitation hold to the ideal of practicing the same spiritual and material charity toward men that Our Lady practiced in the house of St. Elizabeth.

One should say the same for the charity practiced by Our Lady at the marriage feast in Cana. It is an exquisite form of charity to go to the help of others in advance, before they find themselves in trouble and embarrassment. Our Lady did this at Cana. The saints have imitated this example on both little and big occasions. Some have even founded certain institutions for the purpose of saving people from danger and ruin.

For example, St. Antoninus founded an institution for assisting girls who had no dowry for marriage. Thus he rescued many from the danger of vice.

When the Little Flower noticed that another sister had to undertake an especially burdensome task, she managed to get a summons to assist, so as to prevent her from being overworked.

What shall we say of Our Lady's charity on Calvary, where she was willing to see her Son slain for the sake of us sinners? *"Greater love than this no man hath, that a man lay down his life for his friends"* (Jn 15:13). Our Lady would have greatly preferred, many times over, to take her Son's place. She, in fact, consented to feel the most terrible sufferings of Jesus' physical Crucifixion, all for our sake. She could not have been more generous with us.

One example can be mentioned here of imitating Mary's charity. It is the example of one willing to be called "a fool for the Immaculate," St. Maximilian M. Kolbe. Our Lady's heroic charity inflamed him to perform a supreme act of generosity in the concentration camp of Auschwitz, when he asked to take the place of a condemned man and went to die in his place in a starvation bunker. There, he gave spiritual assistance to nine unfortunate companions, praying with them and entrusting them to the holy Virgin as they met their end. True love for Our Lady always produces boundless love for our brother.

The Church's liturgy, borrowing from Ecclesiasticus 24:24, calls Our Lady *"Mother of fair love,"* and observes a feast to honor her Dolors, that is, the loving sacrifice she made of herself in company with Jesus when He was crucified. The fullness of grace and the fullness of sorrow brought Our Lady's love for God to its peak. That is why St. Gemma Galgani once, boldly, and without reserve, ventured to ask Jesus in a transport, to enable her to love Him "as much as Your Mother did." Now this is the supreme summit!

Bear in mind that Our Lady represents the peak of every spiritual perfection; she is imbued with God who *"is charity"* (I Jn 4:16). St. Maximilian wisely stated, "We can affirm with full assurance that the Immaculate is our ideal. Man cannot rise any higher. The Immaculate has the highest degree of perfection and sanctity attainable by a creature. It is a height that no other human creature can reach."

Let us aspire after this *Summit.*

"I am the Mother of fair love."

(Ec 24:24)

Chapter IV

WHAT PRACTICES BELONG TO DEVOTION TO OUR LADY?

- ◆ Consecration to Mary

- ◆ The Holy Rosary

- ◆ The Five and the Fifteen Saturdays

- ◆ The Three Hail Marys

- ◆ The Angelus

- ◆ The Miraculous Medal

- ◆ The Marian Scapular

- ◆ Saturdays devoted to Mary

- ◆ May and October devoted to Mary

PRACTICES OF DEVOTION

Devotion to Our Lady is like a garden full of blossoming flowerbeds, where every bed produces lovely, fragrant blooms. The variety of color and form of the petals and leaves give a charming loveliness to every flowerbed and to the total garden arrangement.

Every devotional practice is like a flowerbed of love for Our Lady. There are so many of them! It is impossible to describe them all. We will limit ourselves to those that are most important and best known to the faithful.

Consecration to Mary

Consecration to Our Lady is a very beautiful and serious commitment and exercise of love. Therefore one must not treat such a sacred thing lightly. The consecration should be made rather with worthy preparation and fully engaged effort.

By this consecration, one offers himself wholly to Our Lady, so that in all he does and undergoes, he depends on her. If it is made as it should be, this consecration achieves a complete surrender of self into Our Lady's hands. From the moment of consecration, she is to enter the life of the person in order to completely Marianize it — to transform it according to her ways. The consecrated person ought to succeed in "living with Mary, for Mary, in Mary," as St. Louis Montfort teaches. But how many are there who truly practice and live their Marian consecration in this way?

There are two kinds of consecration to Our Lady:

1) *Simple* consecration: This is one that is made privately, or in some pious Marian association (as the Daughters of Mary, the Legion of Mary, the Militia of the Immaculate), and it entails a generous and fervent, individual apostolate.

The consecration of families (strongly recommended by St. Gregory), of children (even before birth), of a school, a town, of a nation, etc., belong also to this kind of consecration.

2) Consecration of ourselves as *slaves* of Mary, or as her *property,* or as a *victim in a total sacrifice of love for her*:

The consecration of oneself as a slave is taught by St. Louis de Montfort, and it expresses principally the sacrifice of one's liberty in order to live fettered and ruled by love for Our Lady.

Consecration of oneself as her *property* was taught by St. Maximilian M. Kolbe, and this principally expresses an unconditional surrender of oneself into Mary's immaculate hands as her *instrument or property.*

The other form of consecration is inspired by the Little Flower's offering of herself as a victim of Jesus' merciful love, and it expresses principally the total immolation, the complete sacrifice, of oneself to God, to become like Mary when she totally sacrificed herself in the exercise of generous, merciful love.

Identical in substance, each of these forms of consecration is intended to make us carry out a filial devotion to Our Lady in the most deep-rooted, radical way. They mean to make us sink our roots into Mary's Heart with the happy certainty that "he who plants his roots in Mary becomes holy" (St. Bonaventure). The experience the saints have had assures us that this is quite true.

The Holy Rosary

The Rosary is the precious chain that links us to Mary. It keeps us united to her by the sweet repetition of the Hail Mary while we think about the heavenly Mother with Jesus in the fifteen scenes that make up the Joyful, Sorrowful, and Glorious Mysteries.

The Rosary is love's bond, it is love's welcome, it is love's respite, in which we tell Our Lady many times over, "I love you, I love you, I love you." To clasp our beads is like clasping Our Lady's hand. Also, it is like offering, one by one, a bundle of roses to our sweet Mother and Queen.

The Rosary can be recited by everyone, old and young, learned and unlearned. Any time and place can be suited to reciting the Rosary. Think about the three little shepherds of Fatima, Jacinta, Francisco and Lucia, humble and eager in saying many Rosaries, whether out in the pastures or at home, whether in good health or sick. We recall the Servant of God, Father Anselm M. Treves, who recited Rosaries everywhere, and said many of them "to satisfy his hunger for the Hail Mary" and to "sow Hail Marys" along the highways. Worth remembering is the Servant of God, Giacomino Gaglione, with a Rosary always around his neck, a visible sign of his fervent devotion. Recall, also, the Servant of God, Don Dolindo Ruotolo, always with the Rosary in his hands, whether in church, or in his house, or in the pulpit, or on the street.

Any place is good for saying the Rosary; but the ideal place is before the tabernacle or before Our Lady's altar. One should not forget about the **plenary Indulgence** to be gained when reciting the Rosary in church or with family or in a group, provided one goes to Confession and holy Communion.

Any worthy occasion, circumstance, or cause is suitable for the Rosary — times of joy, times of sorrow, times of success or of failure, when seeking bodily or spiritual health, when one wants to ask graces, or to give thanks, or seek the salvation of souls, or seek the deliverance of souls from Purgatory. Sister Lucia of Fatima said, "From the moment that Our Lady gave importance to the Rosary, there is no problem, material or spiritual, national or international, which cannot be solved."

Therefore, the saints have been fervent lovers of the Rosary. It would seem that they found no better means to express their ardent devotion for Our Lady. Ever since Our Lady gave the Rosary to the human race, saints of old as well as modern Saints have not only taken pains to recite it themselves, but they have made every effort to get others to say it too.

Consider St. Paschal Baylon, who used to make Rosary beads out of cords, putting in knots for the Hail Marys. He would give them away to people to entice them to recite the Rosary.

St. Pompilio Pirrotti was so devoted to the holy Rosary that the quantity he made was a miracle in itself. It was commonly known that he worked at night in company with Our Lady so as produce this huge supply of Rosary beads which he would, in turn, give away; and one night, someone even managed to observe this heavenly scene through a keyhole.

The Curé of Ars' last act, when he was on his deathbed, was to give a Rosary to someone.

We need to mention also St. Alphonsus Liguori, St. Anthony M. Claret, Bl. Bartolo Longo, and many others who were lovers of the Rosary. And let us recall St. Pio of Pietrelcina, the humble but great Capuchin, who used to say up to a hundred Rosaries and more every day, who passed out countless numbers of them to the faithful, and who left his spiritual children the Rosary as their "inheritance," which he entrusted to them before his death with the words, "Always recite the Rosary."

Following Our Lady's counsel at Lourdes and Fatima, and following the example of so many saints, let us also take upon ourselves the daily task of giving at least a quarter of an hour (how little that is!) to saying a Rosary. It would be giving up a quarter of an hour every day for love of Our Lady, a quarter of an hour for the sake of grace for our soul. It would be better yet if we said the Rosary along with others, especially with our family, as Pope Paul VI strongly recommended. We might then see the whole family united in their love for Our Lady, gathered under her mantle, as was the family of Bl. Anna Maria Taigi.

Precious is the advice of Pope Paul VI that we link the Rosary with the Liturgy, using the Rosary, for example, as a preparation and as a thanksgiving for holy Mass and holy Communion. This was the practice of St. Pio of Pietrelcina, who would get up when it was still night to prepare for holy Mass by reciting many Rosaries.

Consider how fitting and effective the Sorrowful Mysteries are as a preparation for holy Mass, in which the Passion and Death of Jesus are re-enacted; for these same mysteries are meditated upon during the Rosary. Consider how the Joyful Mysteries make a beautiful thanksgiving after holy Communion; for, like Our Lady at the Annunciation, we, too, have Jesus physically present in our souls and bodies. This presence lasts as long as the sacred Host keeps the form of bread — that is, about a quarter of an hour. Like Our Lady, we, too, can adore Jesus, our Incarnate God, within us during that time. And as Our Lady carried Jesus about, we, by our Rosaries may keep Him in our affections when we go home, or through the street, and among men, and to our place of work. And we can, so to speak, bring Him forth by acts of sacrifice, by giving an edifying example of charity, of frugality, of angelic purity, of humility and of detachment — virtues of which the Joyful Mysteries should remind us.

Together with the Rosary, other Marian beads (or Crowns) deserve recommendation too, such as the Crown of the Seven Joys and Seven Sorrows, which have nurtured the Marian devotion of many favored souls.[7]

The Five and the Fifteen Saturdays

Here are two other practices of Marian devotion that are very much cherished. The first, the observance of the five first Saturdays of the month, came from Fatima. Lucia, a principal figure in the history of the Fatima revelations, has told us about it. It was a gift of the Immaculate Heart of Mary, who said at Fatima:

---

7 *Translator's note:* also noteworthy is the "Crown of the Seven Glories" which the author himself has recently composed and promoted. It consists of meditating upon her seven glories (her Immaculate Conception, her Divine Maternity, her Perpetual Virginity, her Coredemption, her Spiritual Maternity, her Assumption, her Universal Queenship) while saying an Our Father and seven Hail Mary's.

"Jesus wishes to establish devotion to my Immaculate Heart in the world. I promise salvation to whoever will embrace it."

Special devotion to Mary's loving Heart had already existed for several centuries. St. Matilda and St. Gertrude were active promoters of it. St. Bernadine of Siena preached it fervently. A notable promoter was St. John Eudes in the seventeenth century, who was its father and apostle in a certain sense. He composed a Mass and an office of the Immaculate Heart of Mary. This Founder of two religious congregations wrote the very valuable tract, *The Admirable Heart of the Most Holy Mother of God.*

At Fatima this devotion gained public approval from the Blessed Virgin. Three points of major significance about the devotion were approved: 1) Devotion to Mary's Immaculate Heart is the devotion particularly suited to our times; 2) it demands reparation for the offenses made towards the Immaculate Heart; 3) it asks the consecration of the whole world to the Immaculate Heart.

Our Lady of Fatima said this to Lucia, "My Immaculate Heart will be your refuge and the way that will lead you to God." After having shown them hell, she said to the three children, "You have seen hell where the souls of poor sinners are to finally go. For their salvation God wants to establish in the world devotion to my Immaculate Heart, and if people do all that I will tell you, many souls will be saved."

On December 10, 1925, Our Lady spoke again to Lucia, who had become a religious Sister: "My daughter, behold my Heart all pierced with thorns which men cause to penetrate (my Heart) at every moment by their blasphemy and their ingratitude. You, at least, try to console me, and let the world know that I promise to assist at their hour of death with the graces necessary for their salvation, all those who, on the first Saturday of five consecutive months, go to Confession and receive holy Communion, recite a third part of the Rosary, and keep me company for a quarter of an hour meditating on the mysteries of the Rosary, with the intention of making reparation to me."

This practice is the gift of Mary's Immaculate Heart. Let us adopt it. It is an excellent way to make filial reparation to our Mother's Heart, and it provides a safe refuge for our souls.

The devotion of the *Fifteen Saturdays* had its greatest apostle in Bl. Bartolo Longo. It is a devotion that calls for saying the fifteen mysteries of the holy Rosary in succession on fifteen Saturdays, and it is to prepare us especially for the two feasts of the Rosary, namely, October 7th and May 8th (Our Lady of Pompei). For each of these Saturdays the requirement is Confession, holy Communion, and the entire recitation of the Rosary.

We should consider this practice of Marian piety as something very wholesome and helpful for soul and body; for it moves us to contemplate and imitate the Blessed Virgin in the mysteries of the Rosary; it draws us to the holy Sacraments, and wins for us great favors, even of the temporal order.

The "Three Hail Marys"

The most valuable Marian prayer in the Church is indisputably the *Hail Mary*. It is the prayer of the Angel (*Hail Mary, full of grace, the Lord is with thee*), the prayer of St. Elizabeth (*Blessed art thou amongst women and blessed is the Fruit of thy womb*), the prayer of the Church (*Holy Mary,* etc.) It is certainly the most beautiful prayer after the *Our Father*, the one most pleasing to Our Lady, as she herself revealed to St. Matilda.

The saints have valued the Hail Mary as a prayer that puts devils to flight, brings joy to the Angels, gives glory to the Holy Trinity, and gladdens Mary's Heart: *Rejoice, O Lady full of grace!*

St. Louis Montfort said that the unfailing sign of true devotion to Mary is a love for the *Hail Mary*. Mary's true clients regard the *Hail Mary* as something very dear and most expressive of their love for Our Lady. Is it not something beautiful to consider that with each *Hail Mary* one gives a kiss to our heavenly Mother?

Besides, no one ever appeals to Our Lady in vain, especially if one does so in the words which God

Himself addressed to her through the Angel, and which the Holy Spirit inspired St. Elizabeth and our holy Church to address to her. Therefore, we ought to keep up the devout custom of entrusting ourselves to other people's prayers by asking them to pray a *Hail Mary* for us. This practice has great value.

St. Joseph Cafasso once gave someone a book on Our Lady, who then asked how much she should pay him for it. The Saint answered, "One Hail Mary."

"How can that be? Only a Hail Mary?" the lady exclaimed in surprise!

"Why the surprise? Is a Hail Mary perhaps too little?" the Saint said. "Do you know that, in a vision, St. Teresa once said 'If I could come back to earth to gain the merit of one Hail Mary, I would do so immediately' "?

The devotion of the *Three Hail Marys* is bound up with the value and the cult of the Hail Mary itself. It traces back to St. Matilda, who received it from Our Lady. The Saint had been worrying about her eternal salvation and had requested the most holy Virgin to assist her in her hour of death. Our Lady reassured her, and said, "I will grant your request. But I want you, on your part, to pray to me three Hail Marys every day. With the first, call to mind the strength I received from the Eternal Father; with the second, the wisdom I received from the Son; with the third, the love with which the Holy Spirit filled me."

This practice is both Marian and Trinitarian. Our Lady is the Holy Trinity's masterpiece. What can she not obtain for us from the Heart of the One Triune God?

St. Leonard of Port Maurice, St. Alphonsus Liguori, and St. Anthony Claret were the greatest propagators of this holy practice, which has also been blessed by Popes. In our times, St. Maximilian M. Kolbe and St. Pio of Pietrelcina have given it strong recommendations. The Servant of God, Don Dolindo Ruotolo, exhorted people to say the *Three Hail Marys* with their arms extended in the form of a cross; for "Our Lady is well impressed when we pray to her this way, and she cannot fail to hear us."

A long, complicated practice of piety might seem troublesome. But what is simpler than reciting three Hail Marys? It scarcely takes even a minute of time. What a beautiful thing it would be to begin and end our day by reciting the *Three Hail Marys*! It would mean offering Our Lady our day and our night, our work and our rest, our sacrifice and our relaxation.

Should we not want to do this?

The Angelus

Another prayer which is a little masterpiece is the *Angelus Domini* ("The Angel of the Lord").[8]

---

8 *Translator's note:* this little prayer recalls the dialogue between the Archangel Gabriel and the Blessed Virgin Mary, her *fiat* to the plan of God, and the Incarnation of the Word within her virginal womb.

The Church invites us to call to mind three times a day the great mystery of the Incarnation accomplished in Mary for our salvation.

The Incarnation of the Word was the supreme event first of all for the Blessed Virgin. Within her, God and the human race were brought back into harmony, as the second era began for mankind, the era of world-wide Redemption.

The recitation of the *Angelus* unites us with Mary each time we say it, who, with her humility, her virginity, her perfect obedience, is filled with God. And with the *Angelus* we, too, can become happy sharers in our heavenly Mother's virtues and sentiments. To achieve this more profoundly, an excellent practice is to add a spiritual Communion united with Mary, in order to become filled with Jesus like she was.

The devotion of the saints for the *Angelus* is very impressive. St. Bonaventure started this holy practice ordering, that each evening, the church bells be rung to recall this heavenly event.

Later, the bells were rung three times a day, and St. Vincent de Paul, St. John Baptist de Rossi, St. Leonard of Port Maurice, St. Alphonsus Liguori, and others, fell on their knees three times a day to recite the beautiful *Angelus* prayer with great fervor.

When St. Alphonsus Liguori had grown old and deaf, he begged to be informed when the *Angelus* was rung. Even if he was out on the street, at the first sound of the *Angelus* bell, he knelt at once to recite it.

Who could possibly describe how edifying this devout Bishop was?

St. Pius X, even during his public and private audiences, as soon as he heard the *Angelus* bell sounding, interrupted his conversation, rose to his feet, uncovered his head, and prayed. Pope Paul VI made his Sunday noon recitation of the *Angelus* a public event, reciting it from his window over St. Peter's square, while many pilgrims participated.

Likewise St. Joseph Moscati, a physician deserving high praise, made the sign of the Cross at the sound of the *Angelus*, and if he was in the hospital, or was visiting his patients, he would invite those present to recite the *Angelus* with him.

Bl. Anna Maria Taigi, mother of a family, was fond of this prayer, and every day she said it with fervor together with her family.

The angelic St. Dominic Savio, even from the age of four, needed no one to remind him to say the *Angelus*. His punctuality and faithfulness in this, reminded one of an angel.

And who could forget Padre Pio's recitation of the *Angelus*? Such great devotion was apparent in his face, in his voice, in those hands joined in recollected prayer!

How fortunate we are to be given such worthy examples! Is there not something here to imitate?

The Miraculous Medal

St. Paul wrote that God chooses humble and weak things to confound the great and mighty (cf. I Cor 1:28).

Our Lady gave us a medal as an instrument of grace through St. Catherine Labouré. From then on, favors gained in connection with it were so great and numerous that it earned the title of the *Miraculous* Medal.

The fondness of the saints for this medal has been very noteworthy. The habit of wearing it around the neck, of kissing it, of recommending it to others, of becoming its apostles — this has been characteristic both of the more famous saints, and of those who are less famous.

Here are some examples on record.

St. Catherine Labouré was a fervent promoter of the Miraculous Medal. During the turmoil of the French Revolution it fell to her lot to care for the wounded and deal with soldiers and people of every class. She never failed to promote and offer the Miraculous Medal to them as a pledge of grace.

From her childhood days, the Little Flower, St. Thérèse, proved to be a resourceful apostle of the Miraculous Medal. In her home there was an unbelieving maid-servant who did not want to listen to any talk about religion. But little Thérèse managed to get her to accept a Miraculous Medal and promise to wear it around her neck until death. On another occasion, when some craftsmen were working in her home, little Thérèse managed to slip the Miraculous Medal into the pockets of their coats which they had left on hangers.

Perhaps the most noteworthy example of one who promoted and fully utilized the Miraculous Medal has been St. Maximilian M. Kolbe. He entrusted the special responsibility of *promoting the Miraculous Medal* to his vast Marian movement, the Militia of the Immaculate. All its members are pledged to wear it.

For St. Maximilian, Miraculous Medals were Heaven's *ammunition*, Heaven's *bullets*, which caused grace to penetrate into hearts. This is illustrated in the following episode that happened when he was a patient at a sanatorium in Zakopane, Poland. We quote from a biography:

"When Father Kolbe was at Zakopane he became acquainted with a certain intellectual.

"Whenever they would meet, he would tell him, 'Sir, you should go to Confession.'

"But the man would usually answer, 'No, Reverend Father. I respect you, but I will not go to Confession. Perhaps some other time.'

"After some weeks this gentleman was about to depart, and came to Father Kolbe to say good-bye before leaving. Father Maximilian's last words were, 'Sir, you should go to Confession.'

"'Excuse me, Father,' he said, 'I do not have time. I must hurry to the station.'

"'Then at least take this Miraculous Medal.'

"The gentleman took the medal… and set out at once for the railway station. In the meantime, Father Maximilian dropped on his knees to beg the Immaculate for this obstinate man's conversion.

"And what a wonderful thing happened! After a very short time someone knocked at the door. It was the same gentleman who had been in such a hurry to catch a train. Standing in the threshold he blurted, 'Father, I ask that you hear my Confession.'"

And who does not remember the conversion of the unbelieving Jew, Alphonse Ratisbonne, which happened in Rome? But it would be impossible to list the many favors and graces obtained by the Miraculous Medal.

It is more useful, rather, to learn from the Saints, especially St. Maximilian, how to widely propagate Miraculous Medals everywhere, by giving them away to individuals, depositing them in suitable spots in stores and offices, or on trains. St. Maximilian kept himself always well stocked with these little weapons, and when he could do nothing more in behalf of the Immaculate, he entrusted to these medals the charge of opening hearts, so that Our Lady might reach all.

As for us, it should not be a costly thing to love the Miraculous Medal, to wear one, and to utilize it as an instrument of the Marian apostolate.

Sometimes we give serious thought as to what we should do for Our Lady. Why, then, not become Mary's apostles by using the very simple means of the Miraculous Medal, which can be given to individuals, or sown everywhere like seeds? We may find edifying examples to follow in St. Catherine Labouré, in St. Thérèse of the Child Jesus, in St. Maximilian Kolbe, and in many other saints. Also, St. Pio of Pietrelcina always kept his pockets well supplied with Miraculous Medals. Whoever visits his cell can see a little table there with a handful of Miraculous Medals on it, which were found in his pockets at his death.[9]

Let us do as the saints have done.

The Marian Scapular

Another means of grace is the *Scapular*, or little garb of Our Lady. There are various Marian scapulars. The one that is best known and most widely worn is the Scapular of Our Lady of Mt. Carmel.

Since 1250 A.D., when St. Simon Stock received it from Our Lady during an apparition, the Scapular of Carmel has had a popularity which has never wane over the centuries.

The Scapular is a pledge of the Blessed Virgin Mary and her distinctive livery to symbolically clothe the souls of her clients so as to prevent them from being

9 *Translator's note:* Let us not forget the more recent apostle of the Miraculous Medal, Mother Teresa of Calcutta, who would give them out by handfuls to all she would meet.

condemned to hell. It also gives us a pledge of being delivered from Purgatory on the first Saturday after our death, or at least soon after death, provided we recite daily the Little Office of the Blessed Virgin, or abstain from meat on Wednesdays, Fridays and Saturdays, unless our confessor assigns us some daily prayers as a substitute.

The *Marian Creed*, which the angelic St. Gabriel of Our Lady of Sorrows wrote in his own blood, contains this noteworthy passage: "I believe... your promise to Pope John XXII, that those enrolled in Carmel [the Carmelite Scapular] would be delivered from Purgatory on the Saturday after their death."

This devotion of the Scapular has continually been proposed to us by the Church, whose strong recommendations make it rank second only to the Rosary. Popes and saints have loved it and induced others to love it; for it is something quite simple and at the same time very rich in supernatural content.

The Scapular, when worn around the neck, is a constant summons to surrender ourselves to the heavenly Mother's kindness and to love her. If it is worn with due faith and good will, it is a sure pledge of eternity offered to all men. At Fatima, on October 13, 1917, it was not without reason that the final apparition which the three little shepherds saw, was of Our Lady of Mt. Carmel with the Scapular in her hand.

Let us endeavor to know more about this devotion and make it our own. Our Lady would like to shelter all of her sons and daughters under this heavenly mantle. The Scapular is the tangible sign, the representation, of this Mother's mantle that shelters us. And whoever is found under Mary's mantle, can never perish. We do not, however, claim that the Scapular will save those who otherwise neglect their souls. It is an instrument of grace; but St. Alphonsus tells how men, abusing this grace, have been deprived of their Scapular, even miraculously, at death.

Saturdays devoted to Mary

One day a week dedicated to Our Lady meets a need to offer her something special and particular in the course of the week.

The Church has always realized this need, and has satisfied it by giving Saturday a special place in the Liturgy, with the weekly celebration of a Mass and Office in honor of the Blessed Virgin.

The experience of centuries has approved this holy custom, which the Christian people, in particular the saints, have loved and cherished. We may be sure that the practice of dedicating Saturdays to Mary finds clients of great holiness, including St. Catherine of Siena, St. Francis de Sales, St. Alphonsus Liguori — to name a few.

The association of Saturday with Mary is found among the saints, even in their loftiest mystical experiences. Every Saturday — unlike other days — St.

Gemma Galgani had an ecstasy that involved Our Lady. This had become so customary with her that sometimes it was only when she had an apparition of Our Lady that she realized it was Saturday.

After the example of the saints, we, too, should endeavor to be particularly fond of Saturday as "Mary's day" — as St. Catherine of Siena called it. Let us hallow it with specific prayers, especially the Rosary (if possible, all fifteen mysteries). Let us not fail to make some personal sacrifice (for example, abstaining from fruit, or from meat, or from smoking). Let us add other acts of veneration for Mary, according to our preference; for example, letting Saturday be the day that we finish an important project, or make a decision, or celebrate a particular event. St. Louis Grignon, as a boy, went to holy Communion every Saturday in a church dedicated to Our Lady, out of devotion to her. We may be sure that Our Lady is the better pleased and bestows special favors during this day consecrated to her.

May and October devoted to Mary

Likewise during the two Marian months of May and October, if we want to imitate Our Lady's true clients, we must not fail to take part in the special veneration that the Church pays to the heavenly Mother at those times.

The offering of two whole months indicates a great love that requires long periods in order to give itself more continuously to devotion and prayer.

We would be unable to conclude this work at hand if we attempted to present more examples of saints, along with their exhortations to celebrate these two months with great fervor. They regarded them as golden months — precious times to give vigor to Marian devotion by regular attendance at religious functions throughout May, and by faithfully reciting the fifteen decades of the holy Rosary throughout October.

St. Maximilian wrote a letter to his brother for the purpose of reminding him of the month of May, and sent him a booklet that would be useful for every day of that Marian month. The letter was intended to inspire him with great hopes of gaining very worthy fruits.

Up until the time of his death, Bl. Bartolo Longo showed unwearying zeal in exhorting people to respect the month of October as the month of the Rosary and the month ideally suited for Marian prayer.

Beyond doubt, these two months are months of grace. The Mediatrix of All Grace has a tender concern for the many prayers that people send up to Heaven, and she cannot allow the voices of those who trust in her go unheeded, appealing to her, offering beautiful arrays of prayers and sacrifices for a whole month.

One May, St. Pio of Pietrelcina wrote his spiritual Father, "Now at last the month of our beautiful Mother has returned… This dear Mother continues to give me her fond, motherly attention, especially during this month."

If people are faithful in their observance of these two months, they can obtain even extraordinary graces from Our Lady, for both themselves and others. And — most importantly — spiritual favors of enlightenment, of renewed strength and devotion, of interior growth, of heavenly consolations, that only the Mother of God knows how to give — these would not be lacking then.

During the month of May, with its springtime loveliness, one can deepen one's knowledge of Our Lady by hearing Marian sermons that are customarily given in the churches, or by making meditations on Mary's wonderful privileges and virtues. "O my Father," wrote Padre Pio, "how well this lovely month preaches Mary's sweetness and beauty!"

During the month of October one can strengthen and deepen the ties of love with Our Lady by devoutly reciting more Rosaries. And, thus, one offers the power of his prayer to serve the general missionary intention which the Church proposes that month for the salvation of all souls, through the intercession of her who is the Mediatrix for the salvation of all.

The end.

ACT OF CONSECRATION
TO THE IMMACULATE

By St. Maximilian M. Kolbe

O Immaculate Queen of Heaven and earth, Refuge of sinners and our most loving Mother, to whom God chose to entrust the distribution of His mercies, I, a wretched sinner, kneel at your feet, begging you to accept my whole being as your property and possession.

I offer you, O Mother, all the powers of my soul and body, and I commend into your holy hands my life, my death, my eternity, so that you may henceforth dispose of my whole being just as you please. O dispose of me, Immaculate Virgin, as you see fit, in order to achieve what was written of you: "She shall crush thy head" — the serpent's head; and "All heresies in the world have been overcome through you."

Grant that I may be an efficient instrument of your pure and merciful hands to make you known and loved by those numerous souls who are lukewarm or have gone astray. In this way do you increase as much as possible the number of your true admirers and lovers so that the reign of Jesus' Most Sacred Heart may extend everywhere.

I will see the achievement of what I ask, O holy and Immaculate Mother, only with your help; for where you are, with the graces that you obtain, there alone does one achieve the conversion and sanctification of souls, and there alone can the sweet reign of Jesus' Most Sacred Heart be established. Amen.

The Academy of the Immaculate Books

Obviously there is a need for good, solid, devotional books on Marian Shrines and Saints outstanding in their love for the Blessed Mother and the Eucharistic Jesus. The Franciscans of the Immaculate are attempting to meet this need and flood the book market with readable inspirational books at a reasonable cost.

All Generations Shall Call Me Blessed *by Stefano Manelli, F.I.* A scholarly, easy to read book tracing Mary's role in the Old Testament through prophecies, figures, and symbols, to Mary's presence in the New Testament. A concise exposition which shows clearly Mary's place in the economy of Salvation.

Totus Tuus *by Msgr. Arthur Burton Calkins* provides a thorough examination of the Holy Father's thoughts on total consecration or entrustment to Our Lady based on the historic, theological and scriptural evidence. Vital in clearing away some misunderstandings about entrustment and consecration.

Jesus Our Eucharistic Love *by Fr. Stefano Manelli, F.I.* A treasure of Eucharistic devotional writings and examples from the saints showing their stirring Eucharistic love and devotion. A valuable aid for reading meditative before the Blessed Sacrament.

Virgo Facta Ecclesia *by Franciscans of the Immaculate* is made up of two parts: the first a biography on St. Francis of Assisi and the second part on the Marian character of the Franciscan Order based on its long Marian tradition, from St. Francis to St. Maximilian Kolbe.

Not Made by Hands *by Thomas Sennott.* An excellent resource book covering the two most controversial images in existence: the holy image of Our Lady of Guadalupe on the tilma of Juan Diego and the sacred image of the Crucified on the Shroud of Turin, giving scientific evidence for their authenticity and exposing the fraudulent carbon 14 test.

For the Life of the World *by Jerzy Domanski, O.F.M. Conv.* The former international director of the Knights of the Immaculata and Guardian of the City of the Immaculate in Poland examines Fr. Kolbe's Eucharistic, spiritual life as a priest and adorer of the Eucharist, all in the context of his love of the Immaculate.

Padre Pio of Pietrelcina *by Fr. Stefano Manelli, F.I.* This 144 page popular life of Padre Pio is packed with details about his life, spirituality, and charisms, by one who knew the Padre intimately. The author turned to Padre Pio for guidance in establishing a new Community, the Franciscans of the Immaculate.

Come Follow Me *by Fr. Stefano Manelli, F.I.* A book directed to any young person contemplating a religious vocation. Informative, with many inspiring illustrations and words from the lives and writings of the saints on the challenging vocation of total dedication in following Christ and His Immaculate Mother through the three vows of religion.

A Month with Mary Daily Meditations for a Profound reform of the heart in the School of Mary *by Don Dolindo Ruotolo.* This little book was written by a holy Italian priest Father Dolondo Ruotolo (1882-1970). Originallly written as spiritual thoughts to his spiritual daughter, the work is comprised of thirty-one meditations for the month of May. The month of Mary is the month of a profound reform of heart: we must leave ourselves and adorn ourselves with every virtue and every spiritual good.

Bl. John Duns Scotus: Marian Doctor *by Fr. Stefano Manelli, F.I.* The famous Franciscan theologian, Bl. John Duns Scotus, even before his untimely death in 1308, was renowned for his defense of the Immaculate Conception and known as Marian Doctor par excellence. This book aims at acquainting the general public with the admirable figure of this Scottish-born friar. It does so, above all, to promote the knowledge and love of Christ Jesus and His Mother, the Virgin Mary, in the teaching and life of this holy theologian.

Saints and Marian Shrine Series

Edited by Bro. Francis Mary, F.I.

A Handbook on Guadalupe This well researched book on Guadalupe contains 40 topical chapters by leading experts on Guadalupe with new insights and the latest scientific findings. A number of chapters deal with Our Lady's role as the patroness of the pro-life movement. Well illustrated.

St. Thérèse: Doctor of the Little Way A compendium of 32 chapters covering many unique facets about the latest Doctor of the Church by 23 authors including Fr. John Hardon, S.J., Msgr. Vernon Johnson, Sister Marie of the Trinity, OCD, and Stephanè Piat. This 174 page book is well illustrated.

Padre Pio – The Wonder Worker The latest on this popular saint of our times including the two inspirational homilies given by Pope John Paul II during the beatification celebration in Rome. The first part of the book is a short biography. The second is on his spirituality, charisms, apostolate of the confessional, and his great works of charity.

Marian Shrines of France On the four major Marian shrines and apparitions of France during the 19th century: Our Lady at Rue du Bac (Paris), La Salette, Lourdes and Pointmain. Shows how already in the 19th century Our Lady checkmated our secular, Godless 20th century, introducing the present Age of Mary. Well illustrated.

Marian Shrines of Italy The latest in the series of "Marian Saints and Shrines," with 36 pages of colorful illustrations on over thirty of the 1500 Marian shrines in Italy. This book covers the topic with an underlying theme of the intimate and vital relationship between Mary and the Church, especially apparent in Catholic Italy, where the center of the Catholic faith is found in Rome.

Special rates are available with 25% to 50% discount depending on the number of books, plus postage. For ordering books and further information on rates to book stores, schools and parishes: *Academy of the Immaculate*, *P.O. Box 3003, New Bedford, MA 02741, Phone/FAX (888)90.MARIA [888.90.62742], E-mail academy@ marymediatrix.com*. Quotations on bulk rates by the box, shipped directly from the printery, contact: *Franciscans of the Immaculate, P.O. Box 3003, New Bedford, MA 02741, (508)996-8274, E-mail: ffi@marymediatrix.com. Website: www.marymediatrix.com.*

For a complete listing of books and CDs from the Academy of the Immaculate please refer to our catalog. Request a free catalog by email, letter, or phone via the contact information given above for the Academy of the Immaculate.

THE ACADEMY OF THE IMMACULATE

The Academy of the Immaculate, founded in 1992, is inspired by and based on a project of St. Maximilian M. Kolbe (never realized by the Saint because of his death by martyrdom at the age of 47, August 14, 1941). Among its goals the Academy seeks to promote at every level the study of the Mystery of the Immaculate Conception and the universal maternal mediation of the Virgin Mother of God, and to sponsor publication and dissemination of the fruits of this research in every way possible.

The Academy of the Immaculate is a non-profit religious-charitable organization of the Roman Catholic Church, incorporated under the laws of the Commonwealth of Massachusetts, with its central office at Our Lady's Chapel, POB 3003, New Bedford, MA 02741-3003.